THE
MAKING OF AMERICA
SERIES

WOODBRIDGE
NEW JERSEY'S OLDEST TOWNSHIP

Presented to
the Bridgewater Library
by the
Garden State Writers Group
in celebration of the group's
30th anniversary

1976 – 2006

WOODBRIDGE AND ENVIRONS C. 1963. Prepared by Victor Gruen Associates for the Woodbridge Redevelopment Agency, this map indicates the position of the township within the greater New York–New Jersey–Pennsylvania area.

THE
MAKING OF AMERICA
SERIES

WOODBRIDGE
NEW JERSEY'S OLDEST TOWNSHIP

Virginia Bergen Troeger

VIRGINIA BERGEN TROEGER AND
ROBERT J. MCEWEN

*Garden State Writers
October 2006*

ARCADIA

Published by Arcadia Publishing,
an imprint of Tempus Publishing, Inc.
2 Cumberland Street
Charleston, SC 29401

Printed in Great Britain.

Library of Congress Catalog Card Number: 2002108734

For all general information contact Arcadia Publishing at:
Telephone 843-853-2070
Fax 843-853-0044
E-Mail sales@arcadiapublishing.com

For customer service and orders:
Toll-Free 1-888-313-2665

Visit us on the Internet at http://www.arcadiapublishing.com

To my grandchildren—Julia Lorraine and Linnea Elizabeth Gullikson, James Walter Lavender, and Trevor Scott, Jasmine Hope, and Keriann Jade Lettieri, and in loving memory of my husband, Walter.

—VBT

This History of Woodbridge Township is dedicated to my six grandchildren, Cassandra, Graydon, Jennifer, Kelly, Nicholas, and Zachary, three of whom live in Woodbridge and are the sixth generation to live in this historic town.

—RJMcE

Front cover: MAIN STREET SCENE, c. 1910. Four teams of horse-drawn wagons have pulled up in front of Philipp's Meat Market and Cutter and Brewster's Store on a corner of N. William Street. For many years Choper's Department Store occupied the first floor of the building, which today is occupied by Castello's Fine Italian Restaurant. (Emily and Margaret Lee.)

CONTENTS

Acknowledgments

I certainly would not have been able to write this book without the help of many people who answered questions, located resources, and shared their knowledge and memories of Woodbridge Township. They include Gordon Bond and James Mikusi of the Historical Association of Woodbridge; Rebecca Buck of the Newark Museum; the members of the Garden State Writers' Workshop, especially Pat Brisson, who grew up in Woodbridge; Michelle Chubenko of the Carteret Historical Society; an unnamed Keasbey lady; James Keehbler, Rina Banerjee, and others from the Berkeley Heights Public Library staff; Toyce Collins, president of the Woodbridge Education Association; Cathy McLaughlin from Governor James McGreevey's office; Pat Moran of Avenel; Hillary Murtha of the Middlesex County Cultural and Heritage Commission; Joan Osrath of St. James' School; local historians George Ryan, George W. Stillman, and Walter Stochel; the many members of the New Jersey History Listserv, including Bob Craig, Michael J. Launay, Maxine Lurie, Linda McTeague, Marc Mappen, David Mitros, Scott D. Peters, Herb Rambo, Paul W. Schopp, Stacy Spies, Penny Watson, and Kevin Wright; and the Woodbridge Public Library staff.   —VBT

First of all, I'd like to thank all the unknown people who took the vintage photographs that appear in this book. In addition, my thanks to Jeff Myers and Frank Premako of Acme Studios in Perth Amboy, which has the expertise to copy and restore old photographs to near perfect newness, and to my friend and fellow historian Ray J. Schneider, the resident photographer of the Woodbridge Historical Association, who is always willing to oblige when a request is made for a special picture. In addition, the many friends and organizations who loaned their photographs and/or patiently answered questions include: Don and Emma Aaroe, Edward Berardi, Gordon Bond, Karen Mueller Carlsen, Anthony Cavallero, Lou Creekmur, Tara Dubay, Sonia Carlsen Fedak, Dr. Mario S. Fiorentini, Robert Gawroniak, C. Malcolm B. Gilman M.D., William Harned, Historical Association of Woodbridge Township, Jeff Huber, Jack H. Jacobs, Jean Kreger Jost, Kathy Keating, Emily and Margaret Lee, Mary Ellen Grace Malague, Francis McGinley, Mary Molnar, Reverend Philip N. Nelson, William Nevil, Ernest Oros, Chris Quinn, Joseph Racina, Robert Rippen, Peggie Roscoe, George Ryan, Ray J. Schneider, Margaret Ann Grace Schoder, William T. Smith, and George and Barbara Wyatt.   —RJMcE

INTRODUCTION

Whether you will be returning to Woodbridge through the pages of this book, learning about the town for the first time, or have simply lived in the township all along, may this story of Woodbridge and the vintage and contemporary images that accompany it reach out to you in many ways. Perhaps you will learn something about the community that you did not know before, or perhaps you will view a photograph that reawakens a forgotten memory. But, most importantly, may each of you who turns these pages come away with a greater awareness of the past and present of Woodbridge, New Jersey, a township that has stood at the crossroads of New Jersey for more than three centuries.

AUTHORS' NOTE — Unless otherwise noted under the photograph, all images in this book are taken from the collection of Robert J. McEwen. The authors have made every effort to accurately identify persons and places in the photographs, but realize that errors may have regrettably occurred.

CROSSROADS, C. 1950. *This famous tri-level crossing with Main Street on the top, the Garden State Parkway in the middle, and the New Jersey Turnpike at the bottom, is the only spot in the state where the turnpike and the parkway intersect.*

1. In the Beginning

History does not exist for us until and unless we dig it up, interpret it, and put it together. Then the past comes alive, or more accurately, it is revealed for what it has always been: a part of the present. —Frederick W. Turner III

No history of a town would be complete without first looking at the natural landscape that creates the physical foundation for the community. The force of glaciers, rock formations, volcanic flows, rising and disappearing bodies of water, and monumental shifts in temperature from frigid cold to blazing heat shaped the New Jersey terrain. Countless centuries ago two mighty rivers, the Hudson and the Delaware, emerged to divide the state from neighboring land masses to the east and to the west, sculpting it into the familiar peninsula that is New Jersey today. And between these two rivers, in the physiographic province that geologists have named the Piedmont Plateau, the township of Woodbridge was born in the 1600s. Since that time the Piedmont province has developed into a highly commercial urban area.

During the countless hundreds of centuries before the Lenni-Lenape Indians or the European explorers and settlers found their way here, deposits of various types of clay became part of the local terrain. These basic materials of the earth would eventually turn Woodbridge into a major industrial marketplace during the nineteenth and early twentieth centuries. According to John M. Kreger, ceramic consultant and local historian, Woodbridge clays can be traced to deposits left by glaciers and bodies of water coming from them during the Lower Cretaceous Age.

The Cretaceous Period, one of the geological time periods into which scientists have divided the development of the earth, also marked the appearance of dinosaurs. At least one of these astonishing creatures did indeed roam on Woodbridge soil and left footprints to prove it! In January 1929, township resident and manager of Hampton Cutter's Clay Works, Roy E. Anderson, who had majored in geology at Rutgers University, and his laborers from Hungary unearthed four footprints or trackways at the site of the Cutter clay pits off Amboy Avenue near Strawberry Hill. Although the New Jersey Geological Survey photographed and sketched the tracks at the time, these footprints, identified as tracks of a large, three-toed dinosaur, were in some way demolished.

Another set of four footprints in the same location was unearthed the following January. Immediately, scientists arrived from Rutgers to identify the findings. Paleontologists carefully cut out one of the tracks surrounded by huge sections of clay and transported it by truck to New Brunswick, where college students created a model of the print.

Two months later, in March 1930, the clay workers were once again startled by the discovery of more footprints. William B. Gallagher describes the scene in his book *When Dinosaurs Roamed New Jersey*:

> This time a host of geologists and paleontologists descended on the Hampton Cutter pit. . . . Plaster caps were applied to the carefully excavated footprints to protect them during removal; four tracks were apparently removed, while a fifth was destroyed in the process. Dr. Barnum Brown of the American Museum of Natural History, the famous dinosaur hunter and celebrated discoverer of *Tyrannosaurus rex*, came to Rutgers University to inspect the find. He identified the footprints as those of a large carnivorous dinosaur and noted that they were the only known Cretaceous dinosaur footprints from east of the Mississippi River, a distinction that still holds today.[1]

WHERE A DINOSAUR ONCE ROAMED, C. 1930. Clay workers discovered the footprints of a megalosauropus in Hampton Cutter's claybanks off Amboy Avenue.

9

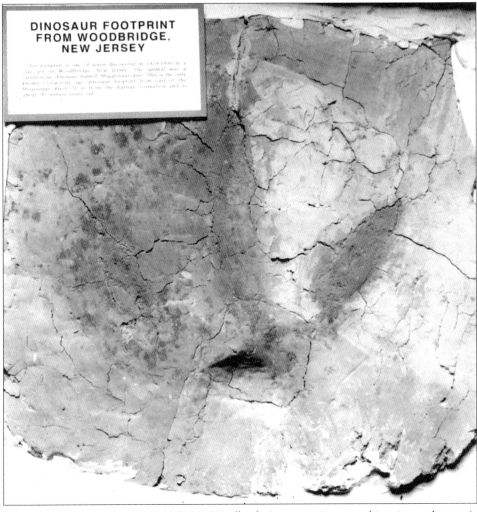

DINOSAUR FOOTPRINT
FROM WOODBRIDGE,
NEW JERSEY

DINOSAUR FOOTPRINT, c. 1930. Woodbridge's remaining pre-historic trackway is displayed in the Geology Building at Rutgers University, New Brunswick, NJ. (Ray J. Schneider)

The New Jersey State Museum had planned to place these last four tracks on display and make copies for other American museums. The plan, however, was never carried out, and these footprints were also lost. Of the nine trackways found in Woodbridge during 1929–1930, only one survives. Identified as a track of the megalosauropus, a meat-eating dinosaur, this prehistoric footprint from the second Cutter discovery in January 1930 is on display at the Rutgers Geological Museum, located in the Geology Building on the College Avenue Campus in New Brunswick.

Gallagher also describes a reconstruction of the trackways by Dr. Donald Baird, former professor at Princeton University:

He [Dr. Baird] believes that all of the tracks were found on the same surface and that they were part of the same trackway made by one animal. They were discovered in the Woodbridge Clay Member of the Raritan Formation, making them about 90 million years old. The preservation of the footprints is due to their original impression into a bed of firm clay, which was quickly buried by a layer of sand. The footprints were around four feet apart, with the midline of the trackway passing through the base of the inner toe prints: this indicates a dinosaur walking upright with its legs tucked in directly beneath its body. There was no trace of a tail drag mark between the footprints, so the dinosaur must have walked with its tail held up off the ground. The footprints themselves were twenty inches long from middle toe tip to the base of the heel. The toes end in pointed claw marks; there is even evidence, on the remaining Rutgers footprint, of a backward-pointing 'spur' or hallux, the impression of the vestigial first [or "big"] toe.[2]

Baird recorded the following:

The most remarkable feature of the Woodbridge trackways is, of course, their preservation in unconsolidated sediments. The footprints were made in damp clay and were almost immediately filled by an overwash of alluvial sand. . . . The preservation of 90-million-year-old footprints under these exceptional circumstances is as unexpected as it is fortunate.[3]

Woodbridge's particular location bordering on the Arthur Kill (Staten Island Sound) and near the mouth of the Raritan River has made it a desirable spot for human settlement from the time of the earliest native peoples. About 10,000 years ago, New Jersey and surrounding areas were inhabited by the Lenni-Lenape Indians whom historians believe migrated to America from Northern Asia. The English would name them the Delawares.

These peaceful people, a branch of the Algonquin Indians who occupied the northeastern United States and Canada, called their domain Lenapehoking, or "Land of the Lenapes." They spoke dialects stemming from the Algonquian language. The name Lenni-Lenape itself means "common people" or "original people."

For many years historians believed that the Lenapes were divided into three large divisions, each represented by a totem or emblem, but more recent studies indicate that there may have been many more sub-groups among them. A Dutch map of New Netherland dated 1650 shows a group of Unami Lenapes, known as Sanhicans (meaning "stone implements") living in the Woodbridge area near the Raritan River. The Unami ("people of the river") used the figure of a turtle as their totem. Scholars estimate that 10,000 to 12,000 Native Americans lived in the New Jersey area during the 1600s.

Primitive in their ways, the Lenapes were a peaceful people with an organized system for governing themselves, a strong religion, and a close relationship with the natural world. Their footpaths and trails which covered New Jersey became the first roads of the European settlers. The closest trail to Woodbridge was the major Lenape trail known as the Minisink. It extended from the mouths of the Navesink and Shrewsbury Rivers to 10 miles south of Port Jervis and passed through Metuchen and Westfield. The Allamatunk Trail, which ran from the Delaware Water Gap to New Brunswick, also skirted Woodbridge.

Seeking a passage to Asia by sailing west, early European navigators thought they had reached India, land of spices and silks, when they landed on the western shores of the Atlantic Ocean in the fifteenth and sixteenth centuries. They called the natives "Indians," an erroneous name that continues in use.

It took almost another century, however, before the Europeans started settlements in Lenapehoking. On a quest in 1609 for the Dutch East India Company, English adventurer Henry Hudson explored the waters of Delaware Bay and the New Jersey coast, and based on Hudson's explorations, the Dutch claimed all land between the Delaware and Connecticut Rivers and called it Nieuw Netherland. They organized the Dutch West India Company in 1621 to import furs, especially beaver skins from the Native Americans. Large-brimmed beaver hats were a popular item with Dutchmen at the time. Soon, New York City's forerunner, Nieuw Amsterdam, grew into a small commercial city on the Hudson River.

The Swedes attempted to colonize in the Delaware River area but were eventually defeated in 1655 by the indomitable governor of all Nieuw Netherland, Peter Stuyvesant. The Dutch themselves, however, were unable to build a strong colony in America. By the beginning of the seventeenth century, Holland was emerging from years of Spanish domination and developing into a strong, Protestant country with a prosperous middle class of merchants and bankers. Few Dutch citizens were interested in embarking on dangerous sea voyages to start over in a wilderness filled with wild beasts and "savages."

Of the three European countries, the Netherlands, Sweden, and England, eyeing the New York–New Jersey–Pennsylvania territory, only the English held on. They wanted continuous colonies from New England to the Carolinas. In 1660, Parliament abolished the Puritan dictatorship of Oliver Cromwell and his son and restored the monarchy in the name of King Charles II, thereby paving the way for the English to close the gap in their American territories.

In 1664, King Charles granted his brother James, the Duke of York and Albany, all land between the Connecticut and Delaware Rivers. He allowed James the absolute right to govern the property. Since the Duke of York wanted to be sure that this real estate windfall was truly under his power, he dispatched four ships commanded by Sir Robert Carr to sail to America and remove the Dutch from control of Nieuw Netherland. James's deputy governor of the Dutch territory, Colonel Richard Nicholls, accompanied Carr on the voyage. While Nicholls was on the high seas, James transferred the territory between the Hudson and the

1656 MAP OF NEW JERSEY. This early Dutch map indicates the existence of the Sanhican branch of the Lenni-Lenapes in the vicinity of the Raritan River. (Robert Rippen)

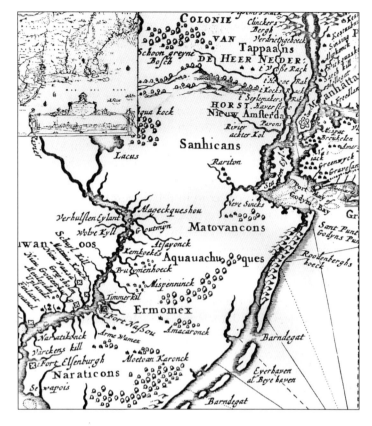

Delaware Rivers to two court favorites, Sir George Carteret and John, Lord Berkeley, and allowed them the right to rule. The Duke of York gave the land two names, "Nova Caesarea" and "New Jersey."

Nicholls and his frigates sailed into the Lower Bay of Nieuw Amsterdam in mid-August 1664 and commanded Governor Stuyvesant to surrender, which he reluctantly did. (The Dutch did retaliate in 1673 and briefly retrieved their territory from the English, only to be defeated permanently in 1674.) No blood was shed in either encounter. After the fall of Nieuw Netherland in 1664, Nicholls thought that the entire Dutch territory was under his jurisdiction, and he took over as governor of Nieuw Netherland. Renaming New Amsterdam New York, to pay homage to the good Duke, Nicholls went ahead with plans to bring settlers into the land west of the Hudson River. He believed that the colonists should tax themselves and offered them religious freedom on a limited basis. All men, except servants and hired laborers, could vote, own land, and hold public office. Nicholls told interested buyers that they should apply to him and then purchase the territory they wanted directly from the Native Americans. They would not be taxed for five years. Because of the lack of communication between Nicholls and the Duke of York, land titles in New Jersey and New York became tangled for years to come.

A group of men known as the "Associates" from Jamaica on Long Island lost no time in presenting a petition to Nicholls to buy land in New Jersey. They had unsuccessfully negotiated with the Dutch for years. The Associates wanted the land west of Staten Island known by the Dutch name of Achter Kol. On October 28, 1664, John Bailey, Daniel Denton, and Luke Watson traveled to Staten Island to arrange with Chief Mattano and other tribal leaders for the sale of the property. Associates Bailey, Denton, and Watson paid 20 fathoms of trading cloth (a fathom equals 6 feet in length), 2 tailored coats, 2 guns, 2 kettles, 10 bars of lead to make bullets, and 20 handfuls of powder for the land. The first permanent English settlement in New Jersey extended from the Raritan River to the Passaic River and some 30 miles into the wilderness. The Associates would make a final payment of 400 fathoms of white wampum the following year.

Denton wrote glowingly of his new purchase:

> Nature has furnished the country with all sorts of wild beasts and fowl, which gave them their food and much of their clothing. Fat venison, turkeys, geese, heath-hens, cranes, swans, ducks, pigeons, and the like . . . and if one chance to meet with an Indian town they shall give him the best entertainment they have, and upon his desire direct him on his way.[4]

In December 1664, Nicholls confirmed the transaction, and settlement became a reality. Other Long Island Associates purchased land in the Sandy Hook area and founded Middletown and Shrewsbury.

Since Lord Berkeley and Sir George Carteret were unaware of Nicholls's transactions, they were making their own plans for colonization. On February 10, 1665, they named a distant cousin of Sir George's, Philip Carteret, as the governor of New Jersey. Philip named the territory Elizabeth Towne in honor of Sir George Carteret's wife, although George and Elizabeth never came to New Jersey. (There were actually two Elizabeth Carterets at this time since Philip's wife was also named Elizabeth.) To the surprise and dismay of Governor Nicholls, who thought he was in charge, Philip arrived at Elizabethtown in the late summer of 1665 to take the reins of his colony, accompanied by an entourage of servants and French and English gentlemen. Twenty-six-year-old Philip joined the Associates and tried to maintain friendly relations in the face of an unfortunate and troublesome situation.

Nicholls complained bitterly in a letter to the Duke of York for giving away the Jersey lands, but the court of King Charles II paid little attention to him. Nicholls governed New York City and vicinity for only four years before he was replaced by Sir Edmond Andros.

After arriving in Elizabethtown in 1665, Philip Carteret presented his constituents with *The Concessions and Agreements of the Lords Proprietors of the Province of New Caesarea or New Jersey*, an official document from John Berkeley and George Carteret. It promised a reasonable amount of self-government, an elected assembly, and religious freedom. The *Concessions* also stated that property owners must pay an annual rent to England beginning in 1670, a clause which angered many settlers, who believed that their arrangements with Nicholls and payments to the Native Americans should exempt them from additional rents.

British settlements organized after Charles II became king marked a major difference in England's colonial policies from the time when colonists migrated from their homeland to New England, Virginia, and Maryland. Many of the settlers who came to New Jersey relocated from Massachusetts, Connecticut, and Long Island, although newcomers from Europe continued to arrive, docking at Elizabethtown. Some historians believe that the Restoration monarchy was reluctant to lose able people whose talents were needed at home, perhaps a precursor of the twentieth-century "brain drain" concerns.

Philip Carteret granted approval to a band of Puritans from Connecticut to establish Newark, and on December 11, 1666 he sold the southern section of the Elizabethtown Purchase to Daniel Pierce and other Massachusetts Puritans. These settlers divided their land into Woodbridge and Piscataway, and thus, the township of Woodbridge, New Jersey, home today to almost 100,000 people, became a reality! (The township of Piscataway had difficulty populating its land and did not officially incorporate until 1798.)

GOVERNER CARTERET ARRIVES. Twenty-six-year-old Philip Carteret and his entourage landed in Elizabethtown in the summer of 1665.

15

By the time of the Revolutionary War, the number of Lenni-Lenape Indians in New Jersey had been reduced to a few hundred. The Europeans brought smallpox, mumps, measles, and tuberculosis to the New World, diseases that quickly killed many natives who had no immunity to them. The newcomers also introduced them to alcohol and firearms, which added to their demise.

In his history of Woodbridge, first published in 1873, Reverend Joseph W. Dally commented that the Native Americans were satisfied with whatever the English offered to pay for their lands and wondered why "the value which the Indians set upon the lands should have been so low."[5] Apparently Dally did not understand that the Native Americans would not have *owned* their land in the Anglo-Saxon tradition of the word. They made use of the land to sustain their lives but never considered themselves property owners holding official deeds and titles. Therefore, the native peoples were temporarily pleased with the coats, blankets, and bars of lead offered by the white men. Only later did they realize that they were no longer wanted on the land that had served as their home for centuries.

In his 1962 book *The Story of the Jersey Blues*, Colonel Malcolm B. Gilman, M.D., a descendent of one of Woodbridge's first families, updated the local Lenapes' story:

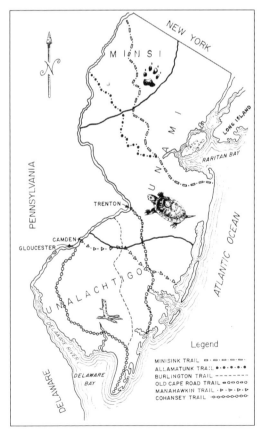

NATIVE AMERICAN TRAILS. Centuries ago the Lenni-Lenapes' Minisink Trail traversed the Woodbridge area.

During the War of 1812 many Lenni-Lenapes, Piscataways, and Rahwac Indians enlisted in the Jersey Blues. These men were descendants of men who formed the Indian Scout Company serving with the Blues in the Revolutionary War. One family of Indians in particular, were close to my mother's family in Bridgetown now Rahway. They lived down along the south branch of the Rahwac River near the Leestown Bridge. Their name was Brown. My great-grandfather gave them barns which were made into houses for their homes. A few of their descendants fought in the Civil War and their progeny are about Union County today.

What happened to the other Leni-Lenapes and Piscataways is less pleasant. Before the Revolution they lived in tribes considerably removed from town and generally along the banks of rivers. After they served in the Colonial Wars they had developed the white man's habits, good and bad. They moved their villages to the edge of towns. This was particularly true at Woodbridge and Piscataway. Some went to church. The Church of Christ in Woodbridge now the Presbyterian Church, and St. Paul's and the Baptist Church in Piscataway. Some even went to the free Quaker school. . . .

After the war of 1812, having served as equals and many died as equals, they began to feel as equals. They worked on the farms, the women frequently worked in the homes . . . By 1820 the early question of integration was at hand. If you read the minutes of the Church meetings you will see how bitterly this was fought. In Woodbridge, family tradition has it, that when the Indians serving my ancestor Gilman's household died, in order to bury them in our plot, they were buried at night.

In 1840 the State Legislature set aside a tract of land of some 100,000 acres in Burlington County for a reservation. The migration began. Few fled into the local forests and hid. A few others remained behind [the Browns] hiding in the homes of their benefactors. The Indians were unhappy down in the pines. They had not selected the site, they were unhappy with the terrain . . . Many hundreds died of exposure and disease. Some trekked back to Woodbridge, Piscataway, and Rahway. Before the Civil War, the Legislature, with the help of the Federal Government, decided to move them to the reservation in Western New York.[6]

Dr. Gilman tells of meeting Lenni-Lenape descendants in 1959 who were selling produce at farm stands in the Lakewood–McGuire Air Force Base area of New Jersey. He found that they knew of their heritage in Woodbridge and Piscataway and accepted their invitation to give a talk to Indian families about their past. When they met a few days later at a local school, Dr. Gilman found his audience eager for information, but he came away saddened. "I could but think, we made them and we broke them. We gave to them and we took it away. Man's inhumanity to man . . ."[7]

But as well-known historian John T. Cunningham points out in *New Jersey, America's Main Road*, the state's first people do live on through their New Jersey place names, such as Passaic, Watchung, Hopatcong, Netcong, Hoboken, Cheesequake, Matawan, Peapack, and Manasquan. In the Woodbridge area, several familiar names have Lenni-Lenape roots. Raritan is a Dutch pronunciation of the Indian word *Wawitan* or *Rarachons*, which means "forked river" or "stream overflows." Metuchen comes from a derivation of Matochsegan, an area Indian chief. One translation of Piscataway, earlier spelled "Piscataqua," may be translated as "it is getting dark." Colonists migrating from Maine may have brought the name of Piscataqua to the local area since there was an Indian tribe and a stream in Maine by that name. Amboy is derived from "Ompoge" or "Amboyle," which has several meanings: "shaped like a bowl," "upright shelf of land," or "able-bodied men." Amboyle was a Lenape fishing grounds. Rahway can probably be traced to Rahwiack, a chief's name meaning "in the midst of the forest." Papiak, the original name of Woodbridge Creek or River, is probably of Indian origin also, but its meaning is uncertain.

The closing years of the seventeenth century marked the end of the Lenni-Lenape's civilization in New Jersey and the beginning of strong settlements of white people. The old order had indeed disappeared as the English carved out their places in the wilderness and transformed forever the land known to the Native Americans.

INDIAN CHIEF. Matochshegan ruled the Matochshoning area (Metuchen) from 1630 to 1700. Joseph J. Perrino painted this portrait from an original sketch dated 1693 and owned by Percy Milligan. The painting was reproduced and given to the Metuchen Library in 1999 by William T. Smith and the Metuchen-Edison Historical Society. (William T. Smith)

2. WOODBRIDGE SETTLES IN

Conquering, holding, daring, venturing as we go the unknown ways, Pioneers! O Pioneers!
—Walt Whitman (from *Leaves of Grass*)

By December 1666, seven towns existed in New Jersey: Elizabethtown, Newark, Woodbridge, Piscataway, Middletown, Shrewsbury, and the Dutch town of Bergen, which later was incorporated into Jersey City. All these settlements were started by strongly independent yeomen with their own ideas of self-government, freedom, religion, and taxation. Each town had a dominant religion. Elizabethtown, Woodbridge, Piscataway, and Newark were Puritan; Middletown, Baptist; Shrewsbury, Quaker; and Bergen, Dutch Reformed.

On December 3, 1667, a year after the New Englanders purchased the Woodbridge tract, Governor Carteret confirmed the purchase with a deed and commissioned Pierce as deputy surveyor to run the boundary lines and lay out the settlers' lands. On June 1, 1669, the town fathers received the governor's official charter granted to the town of Woodbridge. Among its many provisions, the charter gave the landowners (freeholders) the power to choose their own ministers, justices, magistrates, and military officers; guaranteed freedom of religion; authorized a township court; and set aside property for the use of the minister and for free school lands. Churches, schools, and marketplaces would not be charged fees (quitrents). Historians consider the charter, quoted in its entirety in Dally's township history, to be a remarkably broad and humane doctrine.

In 1672, Woodbridge comprised a township of 30,000 acres that extended from Piscataway Township in the west to the Arthur Kill in the east, and from the Raritan River in the south to the Rahway River in the north, excluding the area set aside for Perth Amboy. The original boundaries included the future towns of Carteret, Rahway, and Metuchen; sections of Edison (formerly Raritan) Township; and the communities that comprise the township of Woodbridge today: Woodbridge, Avenel, Colonia, Fords, Hopelawn, Iselin, Keasbey, Menlo Park Terrace, Port Reading, and Sewaren.

Chroniclers of Woodbridge history differ on the origin of the township's name. Dally stated that "the name of the village and township . . . was so called in honor of Rev. John Woodbridge [*c.* 1613–1691] of Newbury, Massachusetts. We presume that this distinction was conferred upon him by his friends and admirers, who came from New England at the solicitation of Gov. Carteret."[1]

Dorothy F.D. Ludewig, author of a Woodbridge history published for the local schools in 1969, wrote that Dr. Gilman told her in a personal interview that Reverend Woodbridge actually came to town, Bible in hand, *c.* 1663. He was accompanied by five men from New England, who helped him build five log cabins and a church meeting house. They went back home but returned with their families to Woodbridge two years later.[2]

Writing for the dissent, local attorney and postmaster Leon McElroy (1896–1958) stated in his "History of Woodbridge" that Dally's information was received from the historian of Newbury, Massachusetts and "is probably in error . . ."

> The Rev. Woodbridge is never recorded as having been in New Jersey and is known to have spent much time in England. The emigrants to Woodbridge were Puritans and were naturally strict adherents of the customs in force in the New England colony of Massachusetts, where the General Court at an early date disposed of the matter of naming towns, by ordering the naming of English towns in New England. Most often the settlers requested permission to use the name of a place where some of them had lived in England . . .
>
> Many of the early settlers of Woodbridge came from Suffolk County, England, about 68 miles northeast of London and in the vicinity of Ipswich. Located about 8 miles from Ipswich is the market town of Woodbridge in the parliamentary division of Suffolk, England. It is situated near the head of the Deben estuary which enters the North Sea. It would be at this point that the people would debark in those days for America . . . Thus it can be accepted that because of the Puritan tradition as exemplified by the Massachusetts General Court, Woodbridge derived its name from its English namesake.

Whatever the true beginning of the name Woodbridge, an ancient English wooden bridge or bridges must have originally inspired both the reverend's surname and the name of the English town. One way or another, the name "Woodbridge" crossed the Atlantic Ocean and settled in central New Jersey.

Arriving from Massachusetts and Long Island, these first pioneers were a skilled, God-fearing group of farmers, brickmakers, lumbermen, weavers, masons, surveyors, carpenters, tanners, and wheelwrights, along with two physicians to look after the sick. Together with their equally hardworking, equally skilled wives who cared for their many children and kept the home fires burning, these founding fathers carved Woodbridge out of the wilderness.

"In 1680 there were 120 slaves in New Jersey."[3] Some Woodbridge colonists probably brought African slaves with them from New England. The Dutch had

BEWIGGED AND BEMUSED. Some historians believe that Woodbridge was named for this pious Congregationalist clergyman, the Reverend John W. Woodbridge of Newbury, Massachusetts.

imported black people since the early 1660s to New York City, the slave-trading center of the area. The larger, local landowners could purchase slaves in the city, or at the port of Perth Amboy, where slave ships also docked.

White, indentured, or bonded servants from Europe comprised another group of laborers for local plantations. Young men and a few women without funds for ship passage would indenture themselves to landowners who would pay their transportation here. In return, the servants would work for their owners for a set period of years. During that time they belonged to their masters but were free when their time was up. Owners rarely freed their black slaves. Usually they remained in bondage for life with their children and grandchildren also born into slavery.

Mary Compton took the honors as the first white child born in Woodbridge township, while her father is believed to be the first white man to chop down trees in town.[4] Mary arrived in the middle of November 1667, the daughter of William and Mary Compton. On January 1, 1696, she married Caleb Campbell. Mary lived into her middle sixties and is buried in the First Presbyterian Church cemetery, where her monument is clearly identified.

As New Jersey historian Richard P. McCormick has written:

> The pattern of settlement in these early years was basically that of the compact agricultural village. The early years of the proprietary regime constitute perhaps the most significant brief period in the history of New Jersey. For these were the formative years, the years when basic governmental institutions were being developed and tested, political

practices were taking form, far-reaching land policies were becoming fixed, and the pattern of economic life was emerging. The course of public affairs was far from tranquil. On the contrary, the proprietary regime was an exceedingly turbulent one, disturbed and even shattered by wars, revolts, and abrupt shifts in English policy. Nevertheless, in spite of discord and instability, the several towns grew and prospered, and the new society took on a distinctive character.[5]

	ACRES.		ACRES.
John Adams	97	STEPHEN KENT	249
Ephraim Andrews (1673)	98	Stephen Kent, Jr	104
Thomas Auger, or Alger	167	Henry Lessenby	88
Obadiah Ayers	171	George Little	100
Samuel Baker, or Bacon	170	HUGH MARCH	320
Joshua Bradley	171	David Makany	168
JOHN BISHOP	470	Samuel Moore	356
John Bishop, Jr	77	Matthew Moore	177
Matthew Bunn, " Mariner "	165	Benjamin Parker, " Joiner "	105
Thos. Blomfield	326	Elisha Parker (1675)	182
Thos. Blomfield, Jr	92	JOHN PIKE	308
John Blomfield	90	John Pike, Jr	91
John Conger	170	DANIEL PIERCE	456
John Cromwell	173	JOSHUA PIERCE	30
Wm. Compton	174	Daniel Robins	173
ROBT. DENNIS	448	Robert Rogers	91
John Dennis	107	JOHN SMITH, " Millwright "†	512
Sam'l Dennis	94	Samuel Smith (1676)	103
John Dilly (1676)	94	John Smith, Scotchman	176
Hugh Dun	92	Isaac Tappan	172
Jonathan Dunham (1672)	213	Abraham Tappan	95½
John French, " Mason "	15	John Taylor, " Blacksmith "	92
Rehoboth Gannit	448	Israel Thorne (1676)	96
Daniel Grasie	164	Robert Vanquellin, }	
Samuel Hale	167	or " La Prairie." }	175
Jonathan Haynes (1673)	97	John Watkins	92
Elisha Ilsley	172	Nathan Webster	93
HENRY JAQUES, }		John Whitaker	91
Henry Jaques, Jr. }	368	Richard Worth	172

	ACRES.		ACRES.
Thos. Adams		Hopewell Hull	
John Allen, " Minister "	97	John Ilsley	97
John Averill		John Martin, Sr	255
Wm. Bingley	186	Thomas Pike	
Jonathan Bishop		John Trewman	97
Capt. Philip Carteret	313	Lords-proprietors	1,000
Jas. Clawson, or Clarkson		For the Ministry	200
Jonathan Dennis		Maintenance of School	100

FIRST WOODBRIDGE LANDOWNERS. *Through the drawing of lots, 57 freeholders received grants of land in 1670. A grant of 100 acres was termed a farm, larger properties were called plantations. In addition to their regular acreage, the nine original Woodbridge Associates listed in capitals each received 240 acres of upland and 40 of meadowland. Names in italics did not appear on a landholders' list of 1682 since they either sold their rights or became freeholders later. (Rev. Joseph W. Dally)*

3. FOUNDATIONS OF FAITH, LAW, AND ORDER

How many goodly creatures are there here! How beauteous mankind is! O brave new world, that has such people in it. —William Shakespeare (from *The Tempest*, Act V, Sc. I.)

The first New England Puritans arriving in Woodbridge in the mid-1660s brought their strict religious beliefs with them. They followed the teachings of the French theologian John Calvin (1509–1564), one of the foremost leaders of the Protestant Reformation in Europe.

Their strongest and most unyielding conviction held that no one was eligible for membership in the church unless he had been personally redeemed by the grace of God. A knowledge of Holy Scriptures and an upstanding life must be accompanied by a true conversion to ensure a place among the elect of God's kingdom.

The Congregational Church in Newark was founded on the severest Puritanical doctrines, making the city a virtual theocracy, while Elizabeth and Woodbridge were started on somewhat less rigorous convictions.

From the beginning, Woodbridge colonists mixed matters of religion with their political issues. As in New England, the clergy was supported by a mandatory tax on all residents. The Freeholders set aside 10 acres of land, known as the Kirk Green or church green, to build a Meeting House, and by 1669 were actively searching for a minister of the Gospel to preach and settle in the community. The committees contacted preachers here and abroad but met with many disappointments. Some had other commitments; others did not want to leave New England for an uncertain financial future in a new settlement. In 1673, Reverend Samuel Treat accepted the committee's offer of 21 pounds sterling to preach for six months but left the township pulpit after that time. Because of a shortage of English currency, salaries, taxes, and debts were often paid in pounds of produce and meat.

With high hopes, the town hired Benjamin Solsbury (Salsbury) the following year to preach twice on Sundays for three months at a salary of £10. But before the first month had passed, he was dismissed. Solsbury was "free from any engagement from this Towne" and "at Liberty to Dispose of himself as he Shall See good."[1]

After this setback, the Freeholders voted to build a 30-foot-square meeting house on the Kirk Green that would serve not only as a house of worship, but also as the seat of government for the township. Perhaps a sturdy building would attract a suitable man of the cloth. By 1682, the Meeting House was still unfinished, and all local menfolk were called to help with the plastering or "daubing." Carpenters made doors and ordered 4,000 lath nails to complete construction. The first Meeting House was plain and simple. High up on the eastern wall was a small pulpit, reached by narrow, steep stairways. A small bell hung in the center requiring the sexton to stand in the middle of the church to ring it. A gallery was added in 1697. Worshippers rented the uncushioned pews by the year. There was no heat since the Puritans considered a fireplace sacrilegious. Churchgoers were permitted to bring foot warmers but were cautioned not to leave them behind after services. When temperatures dropped too low for the Freeholders convening town and court proceedings at the Meeting House, the members moved to the warmth of someone's home.

During the first 15 years of town settlement, the Gospel had been properly preached in town by ordained ministers for a total of only nine months. At last in 1680, townsmen petitioned the governor and council to formally install Reverend John Allen (Allin) as their minister. Although he gave up the pulpit five years later, the popular Reverend Allen stayed in town as a farmer and was appointed town meat packer. Local residents raised animals to sell and needed an honest official to conduct public meat inspections.

INDEPENDENT MEETING HOUSE. The beginnings of Woodbridge can be traced to this modest colonial building where town meetings and non-denominational worship services were held.

Reverend Archibald Riddell, a Scottish refugee escaping religious persecution by the English monarchy, followed Reverend Allen. In 1689, after the furor in his homeland had ended, Riddell went back, and the search for a clergyman in Woodbridge was on again. In 1695, Reverend Samuel Shepard was offered 50 pounds for his ministerial services, a fee to be paid, of course, by the townsfolk. When Quaker William Webster publicly objected to this assessment, John Bishop offered to pay Webster's share for as long as Bishop should live. Five years later the Freeholders voted to raise the minister's salary by voluntary contributions instead of by public tax. In 1702, records show that the Quakers were still protesting, but the steps were in place for the eventual separation of church and state in Woodbridge.

Influenced by the Scottish immigrants, the Puritan or Congregational Church in Woodbridge became a Presbyterian church in 1710 and continues to this day as the First Presbyterian Church of Woodbridge. "Even though the earliest English Calvinists in East Jersey were of Puritan stock from New England, most of them were quietly absorbed into the Presbyterian Church by the time of the Revolution."[2]

The Quakers were holding meetings as early as 1686 in Perth Amboy, and in 1689, in Woodbridge. Escaping persecution in England, many Friends, as they are also called, followed the well-known Quaker William Penn to the New Jersey and Philadelphia areas in the late 1600s. By 1713, Woodbridge Quakers had purchased land on lower Main Street for a burying ground and meeting house. The Society of Friends opposed slavery and war, two philosophies that often found them in conflict with other settlers.

Anglican missionary Reverend Edward Portlock was sent to New Jersey by the Church of England in 1698. He held services in Perth Amboy and Woodbridge but was not as successful at organizing new congregations as he had hoped. He later left the area for Philadelphia to report that East Jersey was hostile toward the Anglican Church.

In 1702, the Woodbridge Anglicans officially became a parish. Prominent resident and town miller Jonathan Dunham and his son Benjamin actively recruited new members. Until c. 1710, the Anglicans attended services at the Meeting House, but left to form their own congregation, the Trinity Protestant Episcopal Church, when the Puritans became Presbyterians. In 1713, the parish started construction on their first church north of the Meeting House, and like the Presbyterians, had difficulty locating a steady minister.

The Roman Catholic faith also arrived early in Woodbridge. According to Leon McElroy, a Jesuit priest, Father Nicholas Gulick arrived from Maryland to baptize Robert DuPoitiers, a ceremony which marked the first Catholic baptism in town. At the same time Father Gulick celebrated the first Mass in Woodbridge at the home of the Frenchman Robert Vanquilion, Governor Carteret's Provincial surveyor in charge of laying out the lands of the province. Until the late 1800s, township Catholics traveled by foot, horseback, or carriage to churches in Perth Amboy or Rahway or met in private homes to celebrate Mass with visiting clergy.

JONATHAN DUNHAM HOUSE, THEN. *An artist's computer rendering shows what Dunham's homestead probably looked like when it was built in the 1670s. Compare with the photograph on p. 28. (Gordon Bond)*

In May 1668, Governor Philip Carteret called New Jersey's first assembly in Elizabethtown and asked each of the seven new towns to send two delegates, known as burgesses. John Bishop and Robert Dennis represented Woodbridge. The first laws passed by the burgesses required men from 16 to 60 to arm themselves and be ready for active military service. Death would be the penalty for incorrigible burglars and those who practiced witchcraft. Other crimes included walking in the dark, reveling after nine o'clock at night, and marrying without proper consent of parents or overseers. The assembly also imposed an annual tax of £5 on each town and instructed the villages to name "fence sitters." These valuable community helpers would be on the lookout for stray cattle that escaped through broken fences to cause damage to crops or become prey for hungry wolves.

The new yeoman settlers lost little time getting down to the business of governing their fledgling community. They managed their local affairs by holding town meetings much as they had done in New England.

The townsmen held their first recorded town meeting on January 1, 1669. Samuel Moore was chosen town clerk, an office he would hold for almost 20 years. He was also selected to be a delegate to the assembly, and the man-in-charge of placing identifying marks on the local horses and cattle. Since the colonists shared common pastures, it was vital that all cattle be identified by their owners.

Because the branding iron had not come into common use as yet, colonists devised various marks and slits as ear marks for their animals. Richard Potter's cattle were marked with three holes in the left ear, while Elisha Parker's stock displayed a cross and a slit on the underside of the "near" ear.

John Smith was chosen constable and an assembly delegate. The office of constable, which may be compared to that of a police chief, was not popular and changed hands yearly so that most of the menfolk held the position at one time or another. In 1686, two constables were appointed.

Town meetings were scheduled to start at 10 a.m. at John Smith's house. Anyone who did not attend was fined 2 shillings, and anyone leaving the room during the session paid 1 shilling. These meetings were not held regularly since the clerk and four others could call the Freeholders together at any time to discuss the issues of the day.

In these early years the town fathers made decisions in many areas of local life. They interpreted and enforced the laws made by the General Assembly of the Province, set salaries of ministers and public officials, determined property rights and settled land disputes, and made decisions about common lands and the building of roads and bridges. In February 1669, the town committee informed residents that they were not allowed to cut down any timber for "pipe staves, clapboards or shingles, except for local use." Forty shillings would be the price to pay for illegal tree chopping.

By July of that year, a border dispute had developed with Piscataway. Officials there accused Woodbridge of claiming territory that belonged to them. Woodbridge disagreed, and Piscataway retaliated by changing boundary stakes, a move that prompted Woodbridge to send a delegate to complain to Governor Carteret. Since notched trees, fence posts, and stakes marked the boundaries, the lines often disappeared or were arbitrarily moved by disgruntled homesteaders. The quarrel rose again and again at town meetings until March 1701, when the Piscataway line was "renewed" to the apparent satisfaction of both communities.

Other issues on the table in 1669 included the designation of a "perpetual Sheep Common" on Strawberry Hill, to be used by homesteaders living on the west side of Papiak Creek, which is the present-day Amboy Avenue and Bunns Lane area. Settlers were also allowed to gather firewood on the Common. Some years later, a flock of geese moved into the Sheep Common and gobbled up the grass intended for the sheep. The Freeholders quickly passed a law stating that any goose seen trespassing on any pasture land would be killed forthwith! Dally wryly noted that in October 1669 the town fathers issued an order:

> granting 10s [shillings] for every wolf killed—the animal's head to be taken to the Constable's house. And this reminds us what a good-natured man John Smith must have been! Did the people wish to attend Town Meeting? They must go to John Smith's. Did they want the Surveyor-General to be entertained? Let him go to John Smith's. Did they want a place to bring all the wolves' heads unto? Take them to John

JONATHAN DUNHAM HOUSE, NOW. This photograph shows the Dunham house as it stands today, with added architectural features. (Gordon Bond)

Smith's house. Clever John Smith! Would that thy hospitality were as frequently met with as thy name!"[3]

The following year found the Freeholders looking for a mill site, a search which apparently did not take long. Woodbridge womenfolk, in particular, must have been overjoyed when Jonathan Dunham's gristmill opened for service:

Jonathan Dunham built the first grist mill ever erected in this part of the country, in the year 1670. The town agreed to give Jonathan 30 pounds for the improvement and all the sod out of the meadow he might need for damming. His toll was to be one-sixteenth, and tradition gives him credit for turning out the most beautiful meal; and we are assured that his toll was so light that a man who brought a bag of grain to him took back two bags of flour. . . .[4]

In 1671, rumors spread throughout the town that the generally friendly Raritan Indians were preparing to attack the town. The Freeholders purchased 10 pounds of powder and 20 pounds of lead, but no attack took place.

The Jersey Blues, the oldest uniformed military militia organization in point of continuous service on the western continent, were organized in 1673 in Woodbridge and Piscataway to control Indians from upper New York and Pennsylvania who came to the area during the summer months for fishing. According to Gilman, these Indians often made a nuisance of themselves, unlike

"Our Indians [who] never give trouble. They work in the fields, help us get the crops in and help us hunt and fish. They teach us how to net Shad and dry them. We are blest with good Friends."[5]

In 1675, the Provincial Government authorized the formation of county courts or courts of sessions as well as the Provincial Court. Middlesex County Court met twice annually, once in Woodbridge, once on Piscataway. After 1686, Perth Amboy was added to the meeting places. The Court of Common Right, or the Supreme Court, established in 1682, met four times a year in Elizabeth. In February 1682, a committee composed of the three Samuels (Moore, Dennis, and Hale) reported to the Freeholders on the organization of the Corporation Court. Four sessions would be held annually with special sessions for urgent cases. They set the fees down to the last shilling and penny to be paid court officers, witnesses, and juries. Jailors' fees were set at 8 shillings for "turning the key in and out," and 5 shillings for affixing the provincial seal to documents. Even in these beginning years the towns were served by an extensive court system, based on ages-old English common law. Whether everyone received a fair trial or not is unknown, but a system of justice that included trial by jury was clearly in place.

In 1682, Jonathan Bishop was granted a parcel of land to build a sawmill along the southern branch of the Rahway River called Succor Brook, located in the future Colonia section of town. The mill would remain tax-free for five years. Early sawmills used huge wooden waterwheels to power the sharp-toothed metal saws.

In 1683, Samuel Dennis and Samuel Moore, the two most popular men in Woodbridge, according to Dally, were elected deputies to the General Assembly and as overseers of the poor. That year must have been an especially busy one for Moore, who was also serving as high sheriff of Middlesex County, messenger of the House of Deputies, township clerk, tax collector, and a member of other township committees. And in his spare time, he opened the first inn or ordinary in Woodbridge and set the local prices for rum. The inn was probably located on today's Green Street near Rahway Avenue. Colonial inns and taverns were not only popular gathering places for the townsmen, but provided overnight accommodations for travelers making the slow and arduous journey between New York City and Philadelphia.

Other township committee business in 1683 included the appointment of three Freeholders to meet with Elizabethtown representatives to plan a highway between Elizabeth and Woodbridge and to report on the town's supply of powder and shot. In 1682, 120 families lived in Woodbridge and vicinity, almost doubling the 57 families who were listed in 1669.

The settlers' belief in public education was clearly stated in their charter, which set aside 100 acres of Woodbridge property (located in present-day Iselin) as Free School Lands, to be forever free of taxation. This acreage was not to be sold to Freeholders but would be used as rental property or money-making farmland with the profits exclusively for education. A schoolhouse itself would not be built on the Free School lands but would be located elsewhere. Unfortunately, records show that the colonists did not make use of the school lands for many years. The long neglect brought squatters to the property and various illegal attempts to purchase the land for settlement.

In 1689, James Fullerton was hired as the first schoolmaster in town. He was followed two years later by John Beacher, who was offered £13 to teach on a trial basis for six months. Next, John Brown of Perth Amboy took on teaching duties at £24 for the year. The townsfolk probably built their first school about 1701 on Strawberry Hill, having used the Meeting House until that time. From the earliest days the concept of public education formed an integral part of the settlers' overall philosophy, but it would be many years before the far-flung public schools of the township were organized under a single board of education.

By the end of the seventeenth century the settlers were fairly well established in their new environment. They had created the foundations for many of their religious beliefs, were holding town meetings to set in motion the laws and practices to maintain their community, had organized a militia for their protection, and were laying the groundwork for public education. And although they may not have realized it at the time, these first English colonists were moving more and more toward a democratic society that would not tolerate interference from the English monarchy that wished to maintain control over their society.

BLOOMFIELD HOUSE. *Dr. Moses Bloomfield of Revolutionary War fame and his family lived in this house, which still stands at 115–117 Harrell Avenue.*

4. WOODBRIDGE IN A WIDER WORLD: 1700–1774

Give me the liberty to know, to enter, and to argue freely according to conscience, above all liberties. —John Milton (from *Areopagitica*, Milton's plea for freedom of the press to the English Parliament in 1644)

By the end of the seventeenth century, local colonists had established a sense of community and order in their wilderness. Many were surely content with their land holdings and the freedom to worship that had brought them here. All lived, however, in constant fear of illness and death, especially from smallpox, a disfiguring and often fatal illness with no prospect of immunization until years later. Mothers died in childbirth; children died at early ages from various communicable diseases.

Several smaller communities within the township were already sparsely settled and known by individual place names. The Fords area was called by the intriguing name of Slingtail Crossing, the origin of which is unknown. Spanktown, Leesville, and Bridgetown referred to areas of Rahway, which was part of Woodbridge until 1860. Colonia was known as Houghtonville after a family who raised sheep in the nearby meadows.

Around 1700, several homesteading families arrived in the future Port Reading section, which was referred to then as simply Woodbridge, or Woodbridge Neck, while Metuchen, later a separate town, was mentioned in colonial records as early as 1688. The first four New Jersey counties, Bergen, Essex, Middlesex, and Monmouth, were in place in 1675 and realigned in 1681. Woodbridge has always remained in Middlesex County.

Except for those involved in provincial affairs, settlers were probably not well informed about the political events taking place beyond Woodbridge. Their self-sufficient lives revolved around their homes, crops, livestock, and Sunday worship. Whatever goods or services they could not barter from a neighbor, they did without, or occasionally requested from their mother country. But the later years of the seventeenth century found the second generation of colonists involved in a wider world.

Lord Berkeley and Sir George Carteret were struggling with monetary problems that would cause both of them to lose control of New Jersey. In 1673,

LORD CORNBURY. Queen Anne appointed this dubious gentleman to serve as governor of New Jersey and New York in 1702. He spent little time on his administrative duties however, as he apparently preferred parading in the streets of New York City in drag! (The New Jersey Historical Society)

Berkeley sold his land to help pay his creditors, a transaction that brought the well-known Quaker William Penn into Jersey affairs.

In 1676, George Carteret, Penn, and other Quakers signed a deed that divided New Jersey into two provinces, East Jersey and West Jersey. A boundary line running from Little Egg Harbor to the northwest corner of the colony defined the Jerseys. Penn received 4,600 square miles in West Jersey, while Carteret took 3,000 square miles in East Jersey, which included Woodbridge. When George Carteret died in 1680, Penn and his associates purchased East Jersey also. After many new investors started buying shares or "proprieties" in the East Jersey enterprise, it became a corporation in 1684, to be known as the Board of Proprietors of the Eastern Division of New Jersey. The board selected the Scottish colony of Ambo Point on the Raritan River for its capital, a city whose name later was changed to Amboy Perth and finally Perth Amboy. The Western New Jersey Proprietors chose Burlington on the Delaware River as their capital.

New Jersey settlers, East and West, were increasingly unhappy with the role of the Proprietors, especially where taxes were concerned. Though they owned the land, the Proprietors received confusing orders from the British monarchy and were uncertain how to govern. The two Jerseys quarreled over boundaries and with New York, whose leaders believed they should direct New Jersey's affairs. Riots broke out in both East and West Jersey.

The Proprietors continued as the law of the land until 1702, when they surrendered their governments to Queen Anne, the younger of James II's daughters. The two Jerseys became the royal colony of New Jersey with the Proprietors continuing only as landowners.

Unfortunately, Queen Anne chose her cousin, Lord Edward Cornbury, as New Jersey's governor. Bigoted, lacking in intelligence, and concerned mainly with filling his own purse, the gentleman also served as governor of New York, where he lived. He rarely crossed the Hudson River onto Jersey soil, but on orders from his Queen, who wanted the unrest among the settlers stopped, Cornbury decreed that no one in New Jersey could keep a printing press.

Other governors followed Cornbury, some excellent leaders, others lackluster politicians, but they governed both New Jersey and New York until 1738. At that time native-born Lewis Morris became governor of New Jersey alone. At last the colony was free of New York interference but not free of disagreements.

THE WOODBRIDGE TEA PARTY

On the lighter side, Dally noted that the first cups of tea served and sipped in New Jersey took place in Woodbridge in 1730 at a party at the home of Widow Campyon on Green Street. The ladies were unsure how to prepare the tea leaves, which had come from New York. Should it be boiled, brewed, or steeped? After much discussion, they decided to steep the hot drink and serve it in tiny cups along with slices of cake. The guests proclaimed the tea delicious, and history was made.[1]

TEA PARTY HOUSE. The small building on the right is believed to have been the home of Mrs. Campyon, who presided at the first New Jersey tea party in 1730. This photograph shows these vintage buildings on the corner of Green Street and Rahway Avenue after the trolley tracks were laid, c. 1900.

One of the town's most influential personages, the publishing entrepreneur James Parker, established his printing business in Woodbridge in 1751, the first permanent printing press in New Jersey. Before 1751, printers would set up temporary presses to handle specific jobs, but by law had to remove them when the work was finished. Parker's resident printing shop was probably located on his father's land at the corner of Amboy Avenue and Grove Street, the site of old St. James' Roman Catholic Church.

Parker was born in town in 1714. His father Samuel was the son of Elisha Parker, who came from Staten Island about 1675. In 1725, as an 11-year-old apprentice, Parker joined the shop of William Bradford, New York's first printer. Bradford published the *New York Gazette*, a weekly newspaper. In May 1733, when his apprenticeship was nearly completed, Parker ran away. Bradford posted a notice in the *Gazette* of May 21, 1733, asking for information about his runaway apprentice, but the young man was not heard from for the next nine years.

Historians suggest that Parker went to work for Benjamin Franklin in Philadelphia before surfacing again in New York in 1742. Since Bradford had discontinued the *Gazette*, Parker began publication of the *Weekly Post Boy*. Apparently there were no hard feelings between Bradford and Parker over his mysterious disappearance. When Bradford died, Parker wrote a complimentary tribute to his former master.

PRINTING PRESS. *An original eighteenth century press similar to the one used by James Parker is located in the Parker Press Building on Rahway Avenue. (Gordon Bond)*

James Parker printed many issues of the *Independent Reflector* in 1752–1753, a publication edited by William Livingston, who became the first governor of the State of New Jersey. Parker was later forced to discontinue publishing the *Reflector* because British subscribers were angered by some of Livingston's opinions. They threatened to stop their subscriptions and have Parker removed as printer for the Province. With a family to support and debts to pay, Parker could not risk continuing to publish the paper.

In 1757, Woodbridge residents made plans to build a sturdy stone bridge across Papiack Creek. In order to speed the process, townsfolk agreed to contribute time, money, labor, or supplies to the project. Parker's name headed the list with the notation "(subscription illegible)."[2] Perhaps Parker should have printed his donation to the bridge-building project instead of writing it by hand! Other donors included James Pike, four loads of stone; James Osborne, four days' work; Thomas Hadden, two loads of oyster shells; and James Kelly, "one load of Stone if he can."

In 1758, Parker brought out the *New American Magazine*, the first periodical published in New Jersey.[3] The 40-page monthly lasted two years and "was filled with a variety of entertaining and instructive matter." Samuel Neville of Perth Amboy edited the magazine, using the impressive nom de plume "Sylvanus Americanus."

Parker and a partner established a press in New Haven to publish Connecticut's first newspaper. In 1761, he brought out the second volume of *Nevill's Compilation of the Laws of New Jersey* with the imprint, "Woodbridge in New Jersey, printed by James Parker, Printer to the Kings most Excellent Majesty, for the Province." He followed three years later with the *Conductor Generalis*, a guide to the duties of the Justices of the Peace, also published in town. Gordon Bond, a member of the Historical Association of Woodbridge and author of a forthcoming biography of James Parker, believes that history has not fully recognized Parker's important role as a strong supporter of the freedom of the press.

In 1764, Parliament refused to issue more paper money, which New Jersey desperately needed to conduct its increasingly complex business dealings. The colony had been particularly hard hit by debt after the French and Indian War and was nearing financial ruin. The following year the colonists were certainly elated when Parker was authorized to print paper money at his Woodbridge press. A tobacco leaf was a prominent motif on the bills since tobacco was an accepted medium of exchange for payment of English goods, especially in the Maryland and Virginia colonies.

An ominous warning, "'Tis Death to Counterfeit," appeared at the bottom of the notes, which were issued in various English denominations, such as 1 shilling, 6 shillings, and 6 pounds. Parker's paper money was valid throughout New Jersey, but as their trade expanded, colonists needed a common colonial currency. That same year Parker moved his press to Burlington to print Samuel Smith's renowned *History of New Jersey*, a book of 574 pages. When Parker completed the job, he and his press returned to Woodbridge.

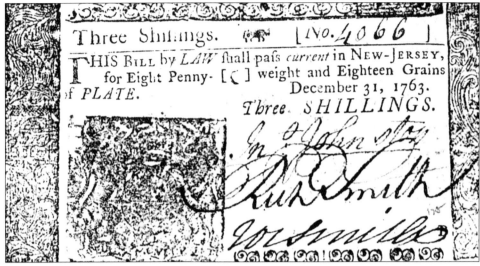

PAPER MONEY, 1763. This bill worth three shillings was printed in Woodbridge by James Parker. (Jeff Huber)

Beside his printer's cap, Parker wore many other hats. He took over Bradford's job as "government printer" for New York in 1745; eight years later he held the same post in New Jersey. He served as Woodbridge Township justice of the peace, New Jersey postmaster, captain of a "Troop of Horse," vestryman of Trinity Episcopal Church in Woodbridge, and comptroller and secretary of the postal department for the Northern District of the British Colonies. While under Parker's management, the postal department operated at a profit for the Crown.

James Parker died on July 2, 1770, in Burlington. Family and friends brought his body to Woodbridge for burial in the First Presbyterian Church Cemetery. His grave was unmarked until October 1969, when the township's 300th Anniversary Committee placed a commemorative marker on his presumed burial place.

Shortly after Parker's death, his son Samuel F. Parker sold his father's Woodbridge print shop and leased his New York office. Sometime during the War for Independence, the print shop was apparently burned to the ground by a band of Tories.

King George III had ascended to the British throne by 1760 and had decided that the unruly American colonists should pay their way and help with England's national debt, a decision that would eventually lead to the War for Independence.

Three years later, William Franklin, Benjamin's 33-year-old son, became New Jersey's governor. The East Jersey Proprietors built a mansion for him, called "The Proprietary House." This landmark edifice still stands on Kearny Avenue in Perth Amboy as the only original existing colonial governor's residence in the 13 colonies. Franklin thought of himself as a worthy servant of a worthy king who understood both American and British problems. But by the time he took office, "the tide of British influence in the New World had begun to ebb swiftly; it would be Franklin's tragic duty to oversee a shipwreck—not to herald the happy voyage of a respected ship of state piloted by King George."[3]

Thoughts of war and active rebellion became a reality in Woodbridge and throughout the colonies in 1765, when Parliament passed the hated Stamp Act. Americans had to buy revenue stamps for legal documents, liquor licenses, playing cards, almanacs, and other printed items. New Jersey colonials were especially enraged because the tax would go toward paying the governor's salary and military expenses.

On September 21, 1765, James Parker denounced the Stamp Act in the first and only issue of the *Constitutional Courant*, considered New Jersey's first newspaper. He strongly denounced Parliament and nearly ran into legal problems because of his harsh protest. Parker's journeyman may have published the attack on his own.

As opposition to the Stamp Act grew more violent, grass-roots groups of men calling themselves the "Sons of Liberty" organized in the colonies. In the late summer of 1765, Woodbridge and Piscataway "Sons" notified William Coxe of Philadelphia, the New Jersey stamp distributor, that if his office was not closed within one week, they would pay him an unpleasant visit. Coxe quickly resigned, but:

> the mere report that Coxe had resigned did not satisfy the Sons of Liberty, and at a meeting held in Woodbridge on the last day of the year two of their members were deputed to secure from the former official conclusive evidence of his resignation. They wished substantial proof of that gentleman's withdrawal, and an impressive missive, which the two

WILLIAM FRANKLIN (1730–1813). The son of Ben Franklin, New Jersey's last royal governor served from 1762 to 1776. (Portrait attributed to Mather Brown.)

deputies bore to him, informed Coxe that should the reasonable request of the Sons of Liberty be refused, they would be put to the trouble of waiting upon him "in such a way and manner as perhaps will be disagreeable both to yourself and us."[4]

The deputies returned to town, drank to the long life of His Majesty George III and Mr. Coxe, and to the resignation of every other colonial stamp master.

Also in 1765, a merchant ship, *Blazing Star*, was built along the Arthur Kill in the village of the same name, which was located in the vicinity of present-day Port Reading and Carteret. The origin of the name Blazing Star is uncertain, but the village, the ship, and a later ferryboat were probably named for the Blazing Star Tavern, which was located near the sound. The English often used colorful, imaginative names for their public houses or pubs. The term "blazing star" was a colloquial name for a comet and would have been in common usage among the English settlers at the time. At first, the vessel transported furniture among the

THE BLAZING STAR. *This topsail schooner, which saw service during the Revolutionary War, was built in 1765 along the Arthur Kill in the village of Blazing Star. (C. Malcolm B. Gilman M.D.)*

colonies. But as the British further limited trade, the *Blazing Star* smuggled contraband, which included applejack from Woodbridge and Rahway, tobacco from Virginia, and tea, paper, glass, and cloth as well as men who wanted refuge from the British.

Parliament finally repealed the Stamp Act in March 1766 but passed the repressive Declaratory Act, where Parliament asserted its right to legislate for the colonies in all cases. There was great joy in Woodbridge when news of the Stamp Act repeal reached the colonies in May of that year. On June 4, King George's 28th birthday, the Sons of Liberty gathered at the Liberty Oak (location not known) with all patriotic townsfolk to celebrate. The colonists presumably drank 18 toasts while enjoying roast ox, plum pudding, and cake, all the while rejoicing with the "utmost Regularity and Decorum, not the least Accident happening."[5]

Trees designated as liberty trees and liberty poles first appeared in the colonies at the time of the Sons of Liberty demonstrations against the Stamp Act. The trees and poles provided central rallying places for nearby colonists and continued for many years as symbols of freedom and protest in America. The Sons of Liberty and other patriots often hung flags and liberty caps on their liberty poles and sometimes hoisted effigies of unpopular figures. The origin of the liberty pole can probably be traced to the English maypole, a symbol celebrating the return of spring, the season of planting and renewal of life, and to similar fetes in ancient Rome.

In 1767, Parliament passed the Townshend Duties on glass, paper, tea, and painters' supplies, which prompted the colonies to enact various Nonimportation Agreements, in which they promised to import no more English goods. Woodbridge merchants announced their own Nonimportation Agreement on April 23, 1770.

Twenty-six people signed the document, which contained six resolutions. First, the merchants pledged their allegiance to King George III, and second, stated that curtailment on colonial rights was unjust. Third, they promised not to deal with anyone violating the Woodbridge Nonimportation Agreement, and fourth, to treat importers breaking the pledge with "contempt and disdain." Their fifth resolution announced that the agreement would be left in force until changed at a general town meeting. Lastly, they named 12 merchants and 12 farmers to a Committee of Correspondence to notify other New Jersey towns and other colonies of their decision. Local patriots meant business. They kept a supply of tar and feathers near the center of town and a ducking stool handy for anyone who might misunderstand the seriousness of nonimportation.

British business suffered from the many Nonimportation Agreements enacted throughout the colonies, and Parliament grudgingly repealed all duties except on tea. For the colonials, however, it was the principle involved, and any tax without representation would guarantee future problems.

After a century of confusion and inaction, Governor Franklin signed a charter on June 24, 1769 in Burlington regulating the management of the Free School Lands of the township. John Moores, Nathaniel Heard, Dr. Moses Bloomfield,

Benjamin Thornall, Evenzer Foster, Joseph Shotwell, and Robert Clarkson became the first official trustees under the charter.

In July 1774, delegations from all New Jersey counties met in New Brunswick to discuss affairs of state. They elected representatives to meet in September with delegates from the other colonies, except Georgia, to organize the Continental Congress. The delegates denied Parliament's right to tax the colonies and prohibited the importation and exportation of British goods with the fervent hope that Great Britain would listen to the colonial grievances.

The period of calm that had reigned throughout the colonies from 1700 to 1773 was over. The Tea Act of 1773 and the Coercive Acts of 1774 propelled many moderate-thinking colonists to join those of a more radical persuasion to move toward active rebellion and bloodshed. Woodbridge patriots and loyalists alike were caught up in the events that would change England's North American colonies into "one nation, under God, indivisible, with liberty and justice for all."

GENERAL HEARD. This favorite Woodbridge son made history by arresting Governor William Franklin on the front steps of the Proprietary House in Perth Amboy in 1776. (Peggie Roscoe)

5. THE REVOLUTIONARY GENERATION

By the rude bridge that arched the flood, / Their flag to April's breeze unfurled, / Here once the embattled farmers stood / And fired the shot heard round the world. —Ralph Waldo Emerson (from *Concord Hymn*)

On Wednesday, April 23, 1775, Woodbridge was shaken by the news brought by a mounted courier heading to Philadelphia. He announced that on April 19th, the first blood of the Patriots had been shed on the green in Lexington, Massachusetts. The British had fired "the shot heard round the world" while trying to capture colonial munitions stores. Suddenly the feelings between the colonists who believed in independence and the Tories loyal to the crown burst into the open. The Loyalists in Woodbridge were ostracized by their once friendly neighbors and looked upon with suspicion. Township Tories were strong in number and vocal in their opinions, but the Patriots outnumbered them. At this time approximately 3,000 people lived in the township, which was twice the area that it is today.

Residents now knew that war was imminent and made plans for active participation. Committees of Correspondence increased their letter writing; men joined local and area regiments and militias. Taverns were crowded each night with townsmen discussing the issues and listening intently to the tales of travelers spending the night. Dr. Moses Bloomfield, ardent Patriot and later a senior physician and surgeon in soldiers' hospitals, announced that the Woodbridge colonists were "determined to stand or fall with the liberties of America."[1]

On June 19, 1776, shortly before the Declaration of Independence was signed in Philadelphia, Woodbridge's distinguished soldier Colonel Nathaniel Heard received orders from Samuel Tucker, president of the Provincial Congress of New Jersey, to arrest Governor William Franklin for remaining loyal to the British Crown.

Heard and a guard of 60 men marched from their barracks in Perth Amboy to the Proprietary House and captured the beleaguered governor on the front steps. Refusing to change his mind, Franklin was taken to Princeton for trial and then handed over to Governor John Trumbull of Connecticut, who held him in prison for more than two years. Franklin's wife Elizabeth Downes Franklin remained in

Perth Amboy for a year and died later in New York. She and her husband never saw each other again.

Heard was later named a brigadier-general commanding, and finally brigadier-general of militia. Since the British were strongly entrenched in Perth Amboy and Staten Island at that time, General George Washington sent word to Heard in July to arrest "any of the Amboy or Staten Island Tories who made themselves obnoxious to the cause of liberty."[2]

Many township men joined the Jersey Blues, who were stationed in Woodbridge, Piscataway, and Perth Amboy. Local members, as well as boys who aspired to serve in the Blues, are believed to have held secret meetings at the homes of Timothy Bloomfield in the vicinity of Fords and Joseph Gilman in Woodbridge. The origin of the name Jersey Blues, which was in use at the time of the French and Indian War (1754–1763), is in question. It may refer to the blue mountains west of Piscataway, the militia's blue uniforms, or to medieval times when knights were bold, and the color blue stood for truth and right. During the Revolution, the members wore royal blue uniforms lined with scarlet, red vests, and tri-cornered, blue-black beaver hats. Buttons on their vests, coats, and cuffs were made of pewter and gilt. The Jersey Blues provided the inner line of defense

Company Officer and Grenadier, parade order

Private, marching order

Light Infantryman

Jersey Blues. These uniforms were worn by the New Jersey regiment before the Revolutionary War. (C. Malcolm B. Gilman M.D.)

at Washington's headquarters at Valley Forge, Pennsylvania, during the winter of 1777–1778. They were also active in Western New York State and Pennsylvania, as well as at Yorktown, Virginia, in 1781, when the British surrendered.

En route to Philadelphia in May 1776, Washington passed through Woodbridge and Perth Amboy. The general was apparently taking the coastal route in order to inspect Staten Island as a place for fortifications. Beginning in the summer of 1776, Woodbridge became a thoroughfare for both Colonial and British forces because of its strategic location. The Americans had lost battles on Long Island, White Plains, and Fort Washington in New York and were retreating through Woodbridge en route to Trenton and the Delaware River. By the end of the year British troops, which included many Hessian mercenaries, were regularly marching through Woodbridge to Perth Amboy and New Brunswick. In early December, the Red Coats rounded up 400 head of cattle and 200 sheep in town. They planned to feed the troops with them during the winter, but a wily militia appeared on the night of December 11 and quietly herded "John Bull's beef and mutton into a colonial camp."

Spirited homemaker Grace Lacky was horrified that Hessian soldiers were entering private homes in Woodbridge and stealing anything they could carry away. She decided to teach these intruders a lesson about breaking and entering. By simply writing two words, "small pox," in large letters on her front door, she was never again troubled by uninvited guests.

As the war moved closer to town in late 1776, women and children were evacuated to mountain areas near Plainfield and Basking Ridge. One resolute patriot, Janet (Jennet) Gage, whose husband, Philip Gage, was a Tory, stayed at home with "no personal fear of the invader." Her neighbors considered Janet's house, which was probably on Strawberry Hill, a safe haven for storing their possessions, while they were in hiding. British soldiers, however, did confiscate some items from the Gage homestead between December 1776 and April 1777 with no record of later repayment.

After losing the Battles of Trenton (December 26, 1776) and Princeton (January 3, 1777), five retreating English regiments encamped in Woodbridge, causing residents to live in fear of plunder and mistreatment. The British were particularly cruel to one family that had two sons in the Continental Army. Soldiers stole 6 horses, 30 head of cattle, and 50 sheep, leaving the family an old grey horse and wagon to make their immediate escape. As soon as they were out of sight, the Red Coats set fire to their house.

About this time the crew of the *Blazing Star* met with General George Washington at the Rahway Tavern. Washington urgently needed more privateers and enlisted the *Blazing Star* into the Continental Army, since the colonies did not have a navy. The Continental Congress had made the act of piracy legal, and the formerly dreaded pirate ships of yore who marauded the high seas suddenly became freedom-fighting privateers.

Continentals and Red Coats fought in several skirmishes and battles on Woodbridge soil during the winter and spring of 1777. After a two-hour

FIRE WAGON. A vintage fire apparatus in Rahway honored the famous Jersey Blues. (C. Malcolm B. Gilman M.D.)

encounter at Spanktown (Rahway) on January 6, 1777, American troops took 1,000 bushels of salt from the British. When the English were nearing defeat, they sent couriers to Woodbridge to ask for reinforcements. Two regiments, probably from Perth Amboy, advanced toward the battlefield, but the Hessian encampment in Woodbridge refused to go because they were certain that a huge New Jersey militia awaited them in Spanktown.

A devastating encounter occurred on February 23, 1777, between General William Maxwell's troops and the Third British Brigade from Perth Amboy. The British had detoured to Spanktown, hoping to capture Maxwell, who held the field. The Americans followed the enemy back to Perth Amboy and fired into the retreating ranks. British and American casualty figures present a contradictory picture of the outcome. The British reported that 4 officers were killed and 100 men were killed or wounded. The Americans stated British losses at 500 men and their own at 3 killed and 12 injured.

In March 1777, the famed British General William Howe was nearly captured in Bonhamtown while trying to open communications with New Brunswick, which had been cut off by the Americans. A serious engagement followed with heavy losses on both sides.

On April 15, 1777, Colonel Cook's 12th Pennsylvania Regiment under Captain Alexander Paterson successfully attacked the British pickets in Bonhamtown, killing or injuring the entire advanced guard of 25 soldiers. British troops took cover in nearby entrenchments.

Continental Captain Lacy and 63 men marched from Rahway through Woodbridge on the night of April 23, 1777, en route to Perth Amboy. They planned to surprise the Hessian pickets there, only to find the guards had moved elsewhere. The following evening, a party of 30 went out on the same mission, but the night was dark and they walked right into the Hessians, who captured them all.

In early May 1777, the Royal Highlanders (71st Scotch Regiment) posted themselves halfway between New Brunswick and Bonhamtown with six companies of light infantry. On May 10, they were attacked and driven out by General Stevens's division of Colonial soldiers.

Grace Lacky took on the enemy once again on May 20, 1777. This time she encountered a Hessian soldier sleeping off an excess of alcohol on the floor of a deserted Woodbridge home. Seeing no American soldiers in sight to help her, she hurried home, dressed herself in men's clothes, and armed with an old flintlock musket, she started out again. Silently entering the abandoned house she carefully removed the soldier's gun and awakened him to demand his surrender. The Hessian sobered quickly and had no choice but to stagger to his feet and head down the road with Grace close behind. The patrol guard of a New Jersey regiment met captor and captive and swiftly took the hapless Hessian into custody.

On June 24, the English forces stationed in Perth Amboy spotted American foot soldiers and mounted troops on Strawberry Hill near the main road between Amboy and Woodbridge. British Captain Patrick Ferguson's body of 250 riflemen and other Red Coats quickly took positions nearby. Ferguson had invented a new rifle that was loaded in the breech or rear part of the bore. The rifle was first used on Strawberry Hill the following day, June 25.

On June 26, 1777, both sides met for a running battle, with the major actions taking place in areas that were then part of Woodbridge Township (Metuchen, Oak Tree Road, Woodland Avenue, Tingley Lane, and Old Raritan Road in the future Edison Township). Since the exact locations of the encounters of the day have not been precisely determined, the battle has been called by various names, including the Battle of the Short Hills (of the Watchung Mountains), Battle of Ash Swamp, and Battle of Westfield.

For several weeks in early June, the British had been trying in vain to coax General Washington's meager army into conflict in central Jersey. Finally Washington led his army down from the Watchung Mountains where he had stationed them out of harm's way. The opening skirmish took place in the vicinity of Routes 1 and 9 near Woodbridge when the Americans met Lord Cornwallis's advancing troops along Oak Tree Road. Colonel Daniel Morgan's riflemen were probably active in this first encounter of the day.

General William "Lord Stirling" Alexander's troops met the English at the Metuchen Meeting House and led the Red Coats into the mud of Ash Swamp in present-day Scotch Plains. English Commander General Charles Cornwallis attacked the Americans with 15 cannon and drove them back to Westfield. Stirling's men lost three cannon in the battle. The British and Hessians marched back to their headquarters in Perth Amboy, while Washington's men stationed in Piscataway and the Plainfields returned to their encampment at Middlebrook in the Watchung Mountains:

> The British strategy to engage the Americans in a major conflict might have worked had it not been for the tactics of New Jersey's Gen. William "Lord Stirling" Alexander's small force who delayed a large portion of the 11,000 pursuing British and Hessians until Washington and his full army of 7,000 troops retreated to the shelter of the Watchung Mountains.[3]

According to local resident George W. Stillman, a Revolutionary War researcher and lecturer:

> The principal achievement of the Battle of [the] Short Hills was that it kept the American forces under General Washington intact, so it could fight when conditions were more favorable against the British military. It also helped encourage British General Howe to give up the occupation of New Jersey and begin his controversial campaign for Philadelphia [the American capital] by sea. He subsequently lost much valuable campaign time in conducting this movement.[4]

The broad area that comprises the Battle of the Short Hills is eligible for listing in both the New Jersey and National Registers of Historic Places as a significant event in American history.

Both sides relied on information about troop movements supplied by local scouts and spies who knew the area. Thirteen-year-old Jonathan Freeman, who lived on the southern edge of the swamp near Rahway, helped the Continentals in the Battle of the Short Hills. He volunteered in Woodbridge to serve as a post rider and scout for the Americans stationed in the area. Freeman was assigned to watch the British in Perth Amboy and vicinity and report their movements to his commanding officer. Jonathan is buried in the cemetery of the First Presbyterian Church, where his grave has recently been given a new granite monument.

Two accounts of war activities in the Woodbridge area involved attacks on British ships. One undated story described that word came to the Jersey Blues, hidden in one of their clandestine meeting places, that a British war vessel had been sighted off Perth Amboy that evening. Someone suggested that the Blues move an aged swivel cannon, affectionately known as the "old sow," to the shore of Raritan Bay and fire at the ship. The men loaded the cannon and attached oxen to pull it to Perth Amboy. Young Campyon Cutter, one of the early members of the prominent Cutter family, planted the cannon on a hill overlooking Raritan Bay near St. Peter's Episcopal Church in Perth Amboy. The men and boys spied the outline of the brig and waited till the moon rose at 11 p.m. At that moment, they aimed their cannon, filled the touch-hole with powder, applied the torch, and set off a heavy detonation. Waiting in silence, the gunners heard the crew raising the anchor, the shot of an enemy cannon that landed in a nearby graveyard, and finally the lapping of water as the ship retreated into the darkness. The British must have thought that their enemy was far greater than a single, ancient cannon.

*REVEREND AZEL ROE
(1738–1815). The British
imprisoned Reverend Roe,
pastor of the First
Presbyterian Church, for
aiding the Americans during
the Revolutionary War.*

On a bitter winter's night in 1780, a party of Continental soldiers headed by Captain John Storey boarded a British vessel that was anchored near Staten Island and loaded with a coveted cargo of molasses and other grocery items. Township soldiers Robert Coddington, Peter Latourette, and James Bloomfield accompanied the captain. Stealthily, they approached the ship in a gunboat, leaped on board, spiked the guns, captured the crew, pulled the precious cargo along the ice to Perth Amboy, and set fire to the ship. The men carried off a cannon from the ship as a trophy of their conquest. For years thereafter, every Fourth of July at dawn, the cannon was used to salute the Stars and Stripes.

Stories of the Revolution involving Woodbridge patriots abound, stories that bring the often far-flung conflict down to a human level where individuals are remembered for acts of courage and determination.

For helping the cause of liberty, Presbyterian minister Reverend Dr. Azel Roe ran into trouble with the British. Together with several of his parishioners, he assisted a company of Continental soldiers in attacking a party of Red Coats at Blazing Star. The British captured him, and he was "compelled for a time to accept the dubious hospitality of the Sugar House prison,"[5] a dilapidated warehouse in the Wall Street section of New York City. The Sugar House was located in the vicinity of the Brooklyn Bridge.

Many men from the Presbyterian Church served in the Continental Army. They included Lieutenant James Paton; Captains David Edgar, Nathaniel Fitz Randolph, Asher Fitz Randolph, Ellis Barron, Abraham Tappen, and Mathias Edgar; Major Reuben Potter; Colonels Benjamin Brown and Samuel Crowe; and General Clarkson Edgar. Outspoken foe of British policies, Timothy Bloomfield was twice imprisoned on the Jersey Prison Ship and nearly hanged twice for refusing to pay allegiance to King George. Both times he was released at the last moment because the British feared Colonial retaliation if he was killed. Thomas Freeman was also sent to the prison ship, but after two weeks he escaped by swimming to Long Island. He finally crossed Staten Island and Perth Amboy to return to his home in Woodbridge, where he hid by day from his Tory neighbors until the end of the war. The British incarcerated many Americans on the Jersey Prison Ship and other such vessels that were docked in New York Harbor. The prisoners were held in filthy, barbarous conditions where more than 11,000 Americans died. Years later, workmen at the Brooklyn Navy Yard uncovered bones of these Revolutionary War prisoners.

While Timothy Bloomfield's sons were away at war, the British ravaged his homestead and stole the precious Bloomfield Family Bible and a brindle cow. Angered at the thievery, Timothy's daughter Eunice and a girlfriend headed for Staten Island to appeal to the British commander in charge of forces there. At the shore they found a rowboat and paddled across Arthur Kill. When the guard on the far shore asked the girls to state their business, they calmly requested to see the commander.

The guard ushered them into the officers' headquarters, where the commander heard their pleading for the return of the Bible. He sent a soldier to retrieve the Good Book from a nearby ship and soon placed it in Eunice's hands. When the young ladies turned to leave, the officer asked if there was anything else he could do for them. Eunice mentioned her missing cow. The officer pointed to the nearby fields where herds of cattle grazed. Eunice stared and stared but could not recognize her animal. She was about to give up when a striped cow trotted over and bumped into her. No one questioned that "Bossy" knew her rightful owner, and a guard of soldiers escorted the girls and their recaptured treasures part of the way home. The story does not relate how the cow fared on the boat ride back to town.

Only one of miller Jonathan Dunham's five sons joined the Continental Army. The others refused to bear arms but helped the Colonials by supplying them with horses that they had taken from the British.

Samuel Dally, a soldier in the first regiment of the Middlesex Militia, left his wife Mary and children on his Woodbridge farm when he went to war. Against Mary and Samuel's wishes, their older son Jeremiah joined up also because he did not want to miss the action.

One day Mary, alone with her younger children, was leaning out an upper window of her farmhouse, watching a skirmish between the Continentals and the Red Coats. The Patriots took the day, and as the British retreated toward Perth

BURNING OF THE PARKER PRESS. The raid on James Parker's former print shop, presumably by the Red Coats, is depicted in this 1976 painting by local artist Francis McGinley.

Amboy, they fired a rifle ball through her window. It struck the opposite wall and fell to the floor. Later, while Colonial soldiers were enjoying a victory drink of Mary's buttermilk, she handed one of them the ball and asked him to return it to its rightful owners. And apparently that is what happened!

Three members of the large Fitz Randolph family held the rank of officer and 27 served as privates in the Revolutionary armies. It is hard to separate fact from fiction, however, in the short life of swashbuckling Captain Nathaniel Fitz Randolph Jr., the son of colonist Nathaniel Sr. "Natty's" adventures add color and excitement to the war years in town. He was bold and intelligent, in apparent contrast to his brother Ezekiel, who had the unfortunate habit of falling asleep on his butcher's cart while making his rounds to his customers' doors. Nathaniel served as a captain in the Middlesex Militia and in December 1778 was elected a naval officer for the Eastern District of New Jersey. The day before his election, the New Jersey Council of Safety ordered the purchase of a sword for the captain as a tribute to his patriotism and bravery. Fitz Randolph and his men were devoted to each other; he turned down a colonel's commission to avoid separation from them.

One night *c.* 1778, Fitz Randolph headed home for a visit. His mother was terrified when she saw him since three armed and mounted Tories had been patrolling around the house that day. After supper and conversation by their glowing hearth, the family heard a sharp knock on the door and calls for the surrender of the captain. Grabbing his sword from a wall bracket, Nathaniel flung open the door and faced his enemies. "I am Natty Randolph," he shouted, aiming his pistol at them. "No three men can take Natty alive! The first who dares to stir is a dead man!"[6]

He ordered the soldiers to move and watched as they slowly and deliberately retreated from the fearless captain, knowing that one false move might end them all. Only when they were sure they were out of Natty's sight did they dare spur their horses and escape into the darkness.

Fitz Randolph displayed feats of cunning and strength on Staten Island when a Hessian shot him in the left arm. Immediately, Natty broke rank from his company, and pretending he had a secret message to communicate, confronted the daring soldier, grabbed him, and triumphantly carried him under his right arm to the Americans. The other Hessians were so amazed that they never tried to rescue their mate.

In another gripping story:

> While at the head of a detachment [of his company] he was once surrounded by a superior British force. Instead of surrendering, the brave fellows stood at bay and fought, under the inspiring example of their leader, *until every one of them had fallen*, either killed or wounded, on the hotly-contested field; and Natty alone, with the blood streaming from his own wounds, stood among his slain companions brandishing a musket with astonishing effect. The British officer, admiring his pluck, sought to take him alive; but every hostile approach met with a stunning blow from the musket. The officer then begged him to surrender, arguing that it was a pity for such a brave man to die. Finding his strength failing, Natty exacted a promise of kind treatment and an early exchange, which being cheerfully accorded, he gave himself up as a prisoner of war.
>
> The promise of the English officer was fulfilled—the American captain was speedily exchanged, every kindness being shown to him in the meantime. The former declared that Fitz Randolph was the bravest man he had ever met.[7]

Alone one day, Natty came upon a British baggage-wagon heading toward the enemy camp. Waiting till dark, he called from the rear of the train, "Come on boys! Here they are! We've got them!" Certain they were in immediate danger, the frightened baggage men fled the scene, leaving Natty to transport his spoils of war back to camp.

Captain Fitz Randolph was captured again by the British in January 1779. Stories vary on how he was actually taken prisoner. He may have been scouting on Staten Island at the time, or he may have been asleep in his bed. Either way he was imprisoned and mistreated in New York for over a year, when he was finally exchanged for a Captain Jones of the British army.

Woodbridge soldier Peter Latourette learned that Captain Jones was ill and staying at Port Richmond on Staten Island. Together with compatriots, Peter traveled to the island in mufti. Assuming they were private citizens, the guard paid little attention to them. After awhile, the Jersey boys heard the sick officer cough and were able to locate his apartment. As the British soldiers proceeded to supper, the guard stacked their guns outside the dining hall. Later Peter armed his men with the guns, entered the captain's rooms, gagged him with a handkerchief, and carried him to their boat. They rowed to Bergen Point, New Jersey, where Natty was imprisoned, and exchanged the British captain for their own beloved and fearless leader.

Two months later, around July 23, 1780, the incomparable Nathaniel Fitz Randolph died at age 32 of wounds he received a month earlier at the Battle of Springfield, New Jersey. Woodbridge's fallen hero was buried with military honors in the First Presbyterian Church Cemetery, where his grave can be seen today.

Although many were active in the war, other members of the Fitz Randolph family were Quakers. As pacifists, the Quakers had a difficult time in Woodbridge during the Revolution. During 1776, their meeting house was occupied by soldiers, and many Quakers were fined or jailed for refusing to go to war, pay the

NATTY'S FINAL RESTING PLACE. Captain Nathaniel Fitz Randolph's gravestone in the First Presbyterian Church cemetery is mysteriously marked by bullet holes. (Ray J. Schneider)

war tax, or affirm allegiance to the Continental Congress. On three occasions Constable Daniel Compton visited Quaker Edward Moore's house to collect his war tax and fines. He confiscated many items, including an iron pot, a table, a hand saw, a square and compass, a cow and two calves. The constable's visit to Jonathan Harned, a tanner, cost that colonist "3 sydes of leather," while James Haydock surrendered "13 chizzles" and a mousetrap.

Quaker strongholds survived in Plainfield and Rahway, but the Woodbridge Friends dwindled in number during the later 1700s. About 1784, they sold their Woodbridge property on Main Street, which was later purchased by members of the Methodist Episcopal Church.

The members of Trinity Episcopal Church were divided between loyalty to Britain and belief in colonial freedom. Although Trinity Church served as a barracks and stable for British or Hessian troops during the war, the Dunham house, which later became the Episcopal rectory, housed local Colonial troops. Numerous Woodbridge Anglicans enlisted in the Colonial forces.

Colonial authorities confiscated the properties of Janet Gage's husband, Loyalist Philip Gage, on August 15, 1778. At that time charges were brought against Philip and others for either joining the Army of the King of Great Britain or offending "against the form of their allegiance to the State." An inquisition was entered against Philip at the Court of Common Pleas in New Brunswick, county seat of Middlesex County. His property was offered for sale when he did not appear in court for final judgment on February 2, 1779. Philip Gage was then branded a fugitive.

CROSS KEYS TAVERN. *Janet Gage raised the Stars and Stripes in front of this early inn, which stood at that time on the corner of Main Street and Amboy Avenue.*

On March 22, 1779, Janet, as highest bidder, purchased two tracts of her husband's property for £900 at a public vendue at the Woodbridge home of Isaac Fitz Randolph. The tracts comprised 53 acres on Strawberry Hill and another tract of 37 acres of salt meadow. Janet would not have been permitted to purchase her husband's property if she had not been a trusted patriot.

Janet Gage holds an important spot in the annals of Woodbridge history by raising the first "Stars and Stripes" in Woodbridge shortly after the Revolutionary War to rally her townsfolk in celebration of their freedom:

> Jennet was determined to have a pole erected; so, taking the black man "Joe" and a yoke of oxen, she went into the woods and selected one of the stateliest and most symmetrical hickory trees. "Joe" cut it down with great satisfaction and trimmed it with care. Then the oxen were brought into requisition and the tree was drawn to the corner of the road opposite Commoss and Ensign's store, where it was set in the ground by Jennet and "Joe." Here the "stars and stripes' were unfurled and gracefully saluted the villagers as the rattling halliards bore them to the top of the pole. This staff was standing nearly in front of the old "Cross Keys Tavern;" but it became so insecure that it was taken down. . . . [Dally describes Janet] as being a woman of enthusiastic temperament and of rather masculine character, but of undoubted patriotism.[8]

Janet chose her spot wisely when she placed the liberty pole at the Cross Keys Tavern. The inn stood on the main post and stage road between New York City and Philadelphia, now Main Street and Amboy Avenue/Route 35. Innkeeper William Manning operated the tavern as a hostelry and town meeting place. When Manning was named the town's first postmaster in 1791, the inn became the first post office of Woodbridge. Today the Knights of Columbus clubhouse stands where the Cross Keys Tavern was located. In the early 1900s the inn was moved to North James Street behind the Knights of Columbus and survives as an apartment building, its history relegated to two roadside markers. The Merchants and Drovers Tavern on St. George's Avenue in Rahway is often considered to be another local Revolutionary War tavern, but recent research places its origin in 1795 or shortly thereafter. The beautifully restored tavern thrives today in its original location as a Union County historical site.

Janet and Philip Gage had four sons, Thomas, Ellis, James, and "big Philip," so named possibly because he was taller than his father was. Janet's extended family tree included an impressive group of historical personages. She descended from Captain John Pike, one of the town's first settlers. Janet and her brother Zebulon were children of James Pike, Captain John's great-grandson. Zebulon Pike served as an officer in the Revolutionary Army.

In 1806, Zebulon's son and Janet's nephew, explorer Zebulon Montgomery Pike, discovered the snow-capped peak in Colorado that bears his name. Zebulon M. Pike also served as a general in the War of 1812 in York (now Toronto),

JOSEPH BLOOMFIELD. Dr. Moses Bloomfield's son became the governor of New Jersey in 1801.

Canada, where he was killed. His daughter Clarissa married John Cleves Symmes Harrison, eldest son of U.S. President William Henry Harrison and uncle of President Benjamin Harrison.

Janet (1748–1821) and Philip Gage (1743–1780) are buried in the United Methodist Church graveyard on Main Street. In 1924, the newly organized Daughters of the American Revolution named their chapter in memory of Janet Gage. The society restored Philip Gage's gravestone and installed a new commemorative boulder and plaque to mark Janet's burial place. It is possible that Janet Gage did not fly the flag of freedom over Woodbridge until 1789, the year of George Washington's inauguration as the first president of the newly formed United States of America. Washington spent the night of April 22, 1789 at the Cross Keys Tavern. He was traveling by stagecoach from Mount Vernon, Virginia, to New York City for his inauguration the following day and arrived in Woodbridge with New Jersey's first state governor, William Livingston. The Woodbridge Cavalry, commanded by Captain Ichabod Potter, escorted the notable visitors to the inn.

On July 4, 1783, shortly after the Revolutionary War ended, a historic anti-slavery meeting occurred in Woodbridge:

> This meeting was held on the farm of Moses Bloomfield, a surgeon in the Continental Army. At the appointed time, Dr. Bloomfield mounted the platform followed by his slaves, fourteen in number, who took their places on each side of him, while he addressed the multitude on the evil of slavery. At the close of the speech, Dr. Bloomfield turned to his slaves,

stating that inasmuch as we as a nation had declared that all men had the right to freedom, he could not consistently undo the principles of the Declaration of Independence by holding slaves. (McElroy)

Revolutionary War veteran Joseph Bloomfield (1753–1823) went on to hold New Jersey's highest office. Son of Dr. Moses Bloomfield, Joseph was born in the old Bloomfield family homestead on Harrell Avenue. He was studying law when the war broke out, but he joined the Colonial army as a captain and later was commissioned a major. He saw action in the Battles of Brandywine in Pennsylvania, and Monmouth. After the war, he practiced law in Burlington and was later elected governor of New Jersey by the assembly and council. Bloomfield was chosen annually from 1801 to 1812, except for 1802 when a tie vote placed the president of the council in charge of the affairs of state for that year. According to McElroy, "No governor of New Jersey has occupied the exalted position of governor for the length of time Bloomfield did." The New Jersey city of Bloomfield remains his namesake.

During the years of the Revolutionary War, Woodbridge committeemen recorded no official business but met annually to select new officers and record new earmarks for township animals. At that time, the town's residents and resources were inexorably bound up in defeating the British, holding their community together through the ravages of battle, and yearning for peace and prosperity. Now at war's end, Woodbridge would stand ready to move into one of the most commercially productive periods in the township's long history.

ZEALOUS PATRIOT. Gravestone on the grounds of the United Methodist Church on Main Street marks the burial spot of Janet Gage. (Ray J. Schneider)

6. CLAY: THE LIFEBLOOD OF WOODBRIDGE

Give me your tired, your poor, / Your huddled masses, yearning to breathe free, / The wretched refuse of your teeming shore, / I lift my lamp beside the golden door! / Send these, the homeless tempest-tossed, to me. —Emma Lazarus (the inscription on the Statue of Liberty, New York Harbor)

If there is one word to describe nineteenth- and early-twentieth-century Woodbridge, that word would have to be "clay." According to John M. Kreger, ceramic consultant, "Clay was the business of our Township. Never again will Woodbridge be blessed with a single industry that employed such a large percentage of its population as did clay."[1]

A New Jersey geologist report, *c.* 1870, outlined the Woodbridge clay area as:

> beginning at the north east on Staten Island Sound near the mouth of Woodbridge Creek, the line runs west, south west, up that creek till opposite Edgar Station on the Woodbridge and Perth Amboy Railroad, which is three-quarters of a mile north of Woodbridge village, thence from the creek running west and southwest near the old Woodbridge and Metuchen road, and intersecting the Metuchen and Bonhamtown road a half mile north of the latter village; thence southward through Piscataway to Martin's Dock, then across the Raritan River . . .[2]

Kreger explained that some parts of this defined area, however, did not yield clay, while other sections held some of the best deposits. The clays found in Woodbridge were of rock origin and traceable to deposits left by glaciers or water coming from the glaciers during the age of reptiles. Kaolin, a fine white clay formed by the weathering of silicate rocks and used in the manufacture of porcelain, was an important local product. It was formed by the weathering of silicate rocks that contain aluminum.

Woodbridge had superior, easily accessible sedimentary clay that produced fire brick capable of withstanding extremely high temperatures. These bricks were in demand for many applications, especially in the steel and ceramic fields.

IN THE DAYS OF CLAY. Clay workers, many recently-arrived European immigrants, stand ready to haul their next loads from the pits to the shipping docks and brick factories.

Although the mining of clay and the manufacturing of products from it did not take top priority in town until much later, the first English settlers recognized the importance of clay and bricks. John French, a dealer in bricks, was granted 15 acres of land in 1670 and was elected a Freeholder with one proviso: he must provide Woodbridge men with bricks in preference to all other prospective buyers.

Historian McElroy believed that the "Molden Men's Lots" mentioned in early records referred to local properties set aside by the founding fathers for purchase by brick makers or men who "molded bricks." Dally reported that white clay from the area was familiar to soldiers stationed in Perth Amboy during the Revolutionary War. They called it "Fuller's Earth" and used it for dry cleaning their buckskin breeches.

At the beginning of the eighteenth century, residents offered their lands for sale with the added incentive that they had clay on their properties. Sellers included Isaac Potter from the future Keasbey section, who advertised 28 acres for sale "with plenty of clay ground adjoining," and John E. and Benjamin M. Noe, who promoted the clay on their 88-acre farm on the Turnpike Road.

The first documented clay shipment from Woodbridge took place in 1816, when a merchant named Price sailed a boatload of fire clay to Boston. In the early days, laborers using pickaxes and shovels mined the local clays; later steam shovels were introduced. Horse-drawn wagons moved the tons of clay to a dock on Woodbridge Creek for loading onto barges and boats.

The Salamander Works, which manufactured such fireproof ware as cupola linings, furnace blocks, slabs, bakers' ovens, and pipes for drains, sewers, and heaters, opened its doors on Rahway Avenue near Heard's Brook in 1825. (The firm's property was occupied in later years by the Woodbridge Lumber Company and is now the Parker Press Park.) Gage Inslee and René Pardessus are believed to be the founders of the company, which changed hands several times through the years.

In 1835, clay dealer Peter Melick sold Pardessus 23 acres of land on the road from Woodbridge to Metuchen to expand Salamander. Two years later New Yorker Michel Lefoulon, a native of France, bought the company and moved with his family to town. In failing health, Lefoulon sold Salamander to Jules Decasse in June 1842. The 41-year-old Lefoulon died shortly thereafter while on a sea voyage and was buried in the Trinity Episcopal Church cemetery.

Salamander became known during the 1830s and 1840s for stoneware that used a Rockingham glaze. (Rockingham was an English pottery company specializing in red-brown and other colored glazes.) Salamander produced several uniquely designed pitchers: a dog-handled pitcher depicting a boar hunt, another showing a side-wheel steamer, and pitchers displaying designs of grapevines, satyr masks, fauns' heads, and scrolls. The pottery collections of the Smithsonian Institution, the Brooklyn Museum, the Henry Ford Museum, and the New Jersey State Museum contain examples of Salamander's ware. Other pieces exist today in private Woodbridge collections.

In April 1850, Jules Decasse deeded all of the Salamander Works to New York importer Louis Decasse, a resident of Woodbridge and most likely Jules's son. In 1867, William Poillon took over as owner and operated Salamander with his son Cornelius until 1896, when a devastating fire destroyed the factory.

Around 1901, Poillon relatives Clara Louise Poillon (Mrs. Cornelius) and Mrs. Howard A. Poillon, who had previously opened a pottery factory in Jersey City, invested in a new kiln at the former Salamander Works and moved the C.L. and H.A. Poillon Pottery to Woodbridge. The ladies' interest in decorating pieces of blank china led to their business venture. "By the 1890s china painting was a national phenomenon, a do-it-yourself craze that hundreds of thousands of women across America joined for pleasure or profit."[3] The Poillons lived in New York City and often exhibited their art pottery at shows there as well as at the St. Louis Exposition in 1904.

Clara Poillon developed high gloss and matte glazes as well as gold and orange lusters to decorate their company's garden and kitchenware. The company later closed its Woodbridge factory and relocated to Trenton. Until the completion of the present-day shopping strip on the site of the Poillon factory, Woodbridge residents unearthed door knobs and small clay dishes from the property. Today the block-long Poillon Street stands as a lone remnant in downtown Woodbridge of the heyday of pottery-making in town.

Hampton Cutter (1811–1882) unearthed a large deposit of kaolin on his farm in 1845, not knowing that years later dinosaur tracks would be found in his claybanks. Digging deeper in future years, he found a strata of fine blue clay, used in the manufacture of fire bricks. Cutter quickly saw his future in the raw clay market and supplied nearby factories and distant markets in New England, New York, and Ohio. His sons Josiah C. and William Henry, as well as his son-in-law James Prall, later joined his booming business.

Cutter was not only successful in business but was also an active man about town. He was justice of the peace for 15 years, served as a member of the Board of Chosen Freeholders of Middlesex County, and was a director of the National Bank of Rahway, as well as holding many offices at the First Presbyterian Church. His family homestead, the Cutter-Prall mansion, thrives today as a Woodbridge landmark in the Strawberry Hill section of Amboy Avenue. The Cutter-Prall house was sold in 1926 to the Little Servant Sisters of the Immaculate Conception, a Polish order of nuns, who maintained an orphanage there from 1928 until 1948, when it closed for a lack of funds. That year the sisters opened the Mt. Carmel Nursing Home on the property, to be followed by the Strawberry Hill Senior Day Center in 1973, and St. Joseph's Seniors' Residence in 1981, all of which are currently in operation.

William H. Cutter followed in his father's footsteps in the clay business and was later succeeded by his son Hampton II, the last of the Cutter clay merchants. William's family home on Green Street, long the residence of his daughter Laura, presently houses the headquarters of the Central Jersey Federal Credit Union, while the Byron Dunham family owns Hampton II's house next door.

SALAMANDER WORKS. Located on Rahway Avenue near Heard's Brook, the company opened in 1825 to manufacture fireproof ware for home and industry.

Maine native William H. Berry brought his hay baling and shipping business to Woodbridge from Jersey City in 1832. By 1845, Berry moved into the clay market and opened a firebrick factory near Hawk's Nest Landing on Woodbridge Creek. His firm was soon producing one million bricks a year. Berry is also credited with introducing anthracite, or hard coal, to the local commercial community.

Public-spirited Berry's list of local accomplishments was a long one. He founded a savings bank, and served as township committee chairman, school trustee, and member of the building committee for School Number One in 1877. At the Methodist church, he presided over the board of trustees for 30 years and acted as Sunday school superintendent. Berry supported the Union during the Civil War (1861–1865) and allowed Union soldiers to drill in his factory buildings.

Henry Maurer, an enterprising German immigrant, arrived in New York City in 1830 at the age of 18 and worked at several brick-making businesses. In 1856, he bought the Excelsior Fire-Brick and Clay Retort Works just over the Woodbridge line in Perth Amboy in a 75-acre section later known as Maurer, and also 11 acres of excellent fire clay banks off upper Main Street in Woodbridge. He invested $50,000 to upgrade his fire-brick factory, which employed about 100

CLAY MAGNATE. Hampton Cutter (1811–1882) made his fortune after discovering clay deposits on his farm in 1845.

men. In 1881, he manufactured 520,000 hollow bricks, and 1,750,000 fire-bricks, as well as gas retorts and French roofing tiles. His bricks were used in many New York City buildings, including several owned by the well-known Vanderbilt family. Maurer, who invented various machines to speed his manufacturing processes, maintained his business office, a depot, and his home in New York City. Maurer and Sons continued operating until 1937.

Samuel Dally, son of Elizabeth Gage and Charles Dally, a weaver and owner of a clay company, did not become a clay merchant until later in his life. He was born in 1810 in Mutton Hollow on outer Main Street, and at age 16 was indentured to a blacksmith. When Samuel came down with malaria, he was released from his bond and returned home to learn the weaver's trade from his father. But Samuel did not long remain at his loom. He changed careers, first to farming, and then to an eight-year stint as a butcher. After his father's death, he took over his clay business and ran it for 16 years at a considerable profit. Samuel abruptly left his firm during the Civil War in 1864, apparently upset by U.S. Army recruiting officers who were offering his laborers large enlistment bounties to join the Union Army. Dally was described as follows:

> Tradition says he [Samuel Dally] was a wild boy, but getting married tamed him. Industry took the place of idleness and earnest business was substituted for profitless vacancy. . . . Dally's promptness in paying his bills led me to believe, long before he had a fortune, that he must be rich. He resolved always to honor God, and never in the family or in business did he compromise Christian principles. . . . An example to young men of the fruits of sober industry and uncompromising piety.[4]

Cassimir Whitman Boynton, another Maine native, opened C.W. Boynton and Company at the mouth of Woodbridge Creek in Sewaren in 1866 to manufacture drain pipe, hollow tile, and fireproof shingles. The company was the first in the Woodbridge vicinity to produce hollow tile that was used in the construction of fireproof buildings. Boynton's factory was demolished by fire in 1881, but a new three-story brick building supplied with power and new machinery quickly rose from the ashes.

Brothers Mulford D. and James R. Valentine started their firebrick business in 1866 at the southern end of Fulton Street. In ten years the plant was producing 4 million firebricks a year, bricks considered by many to be the best in the world.

The Valentine factory was consumed by a devastating fire in 1956, but 11 months later, it was up and running again with modern equipment. The company became a division of the A.P. Green Fire Brick Company of Mexico, Missouri, in 1958 and stayed in business until the last day of 1983. One brick kiln and several buildings still stand on the property and are rented or used as storage by the present owner, the E.E. Cruz Company, an engineering concern from Holmdel, New Jersey. The future of these buildings is uncertain; they may be razed for an industrial park.

The list of burgeoning clay and brick businesses in the Woodbridge area during the nineteenth century and early years of the twentieth century was long indeed. It included the Mutton Hollow Fire Brick Company, Ostrander Brick Works, Melick Brothers Clay Mining Company, Florida Grove Company of Fords, Carteret Brick Works, Federal Terra Cotta Company, Anness and Potter Fire Clay Company, General Ceramics of Keasbey, National Fireproofing Company, Atlantic Terra Cotta Company, McHose Clay Company, J. Flood and Son, Ayres and Company, Raritan Hollow and Porous Brick Company, and G.G. Brinkman Company. Members of the Crossman, Inslee, Dunigan, Drummond, Ryan, and Almasi families, among others, were also involved in the industry.

By the mid-1800s, the many clay-related businesses were attracting job seekers from Scotland, England, Ireland, and Germany, who arrived through the ports of New York and Perth Amboy. A foreman at the National Fireproofing Company in Keasbey learned five languages so that he might communicate with his diverse workers. The devastating potato famine in Ireland in 1846 and later economic downturns brought thousands of Irish immigrants to America's shores and ultimately to Woodbridge.

Andrew Gerity and his wife Mary Jane Bolan Gerity, both natives of Ireland, are representative of the families who came at this time. Andrew built a four-room house for $900 in 1871 on Fulton Street near Albert Street. He was employed as a gate tender on the Central Railroad drawbridge between Sewaren and the Maurer section of Perth Amboy. He worked 12 hours a day and received $36 for 30 days of work. The Geritys built several more houses in the vicinity, including one with a grocery storefront. As the years passed, their neighbors, who included the Mooney, Finn, Mullen, and Shannon families, nicknamed Albert Street "Gerity's Corner." In October 1892, Andrew, age 52, was killed by a train while on the job.

Several of Mary Jane and Andrew's nine children settled in Woodbridge. William Henry, nicknamed "Tuts," worked in several firebrick factories, where he built kilns and furnaces. James founded the real estate and insurance firm J.P. Gerity and Company in the Gerity Building at 21 Main Street. The Gerity family was active in St. James Church, the Knights of Columbus, and in local politics. After World War II, grandson Leon Joseph Gerity opened the Leon J. Gerity Funeral Home on Amboy Avenue. When Leon retired, his daughters Susan Fox and Mary Ann Sullivan, both funeral directors, continued the business, which remains in its original location. Great-granddaughter Pat Brisson, daughter of Jane M. Gerity and Thomas McDonough, grew up in Woodbridge and is an award-winning author of children's books. Members of the Gerity family have lived and worked in Woodbridge for more than 125 years.

Political unrest in the Scandinavian countries brought Swedish immigrants Hannah Larsen and Axel Frederick Nelson to New York on separate ships in the 1880s. Hannah was registered by a recruiter looking for young women to be employed as housemaids. She found her way to Woodbridge to work for the Prall family on Strawberry Hill. Axel was not picked up by a recruiter but spotted a

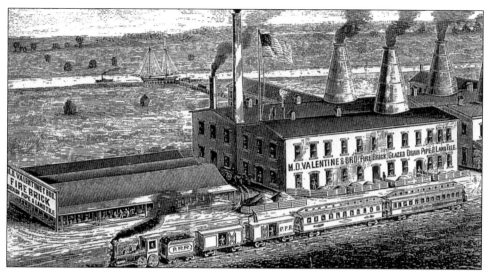

M.D. VALENTINE & BRO. Mulford D. and James R. Valentine strategically located their brick works on Fulton Street near Woodbridge Creek and the Pennsylvania Railroad.

small ship loaded with barrels of pickled pigs' feet and inquired where it was going. Woodbridge was its destination. Axel boarded the ship and found his new job digging clay at Prall's claybanks. When he turned up at the back door of the Prall homestead to collect his pay, Hannah opened the door, and a romance blossomed.

Hannah and Axel were married in 1886 at the Lutheran Church in Perth Amboy and had six children. Their son Frederick Axel married Etta Noe, a descendent of one of the town's colonial families. Her father managed the Central Hotel on Main Street, near the Williams Street corner, while her mother worked as the hotel's housekeeper. Fred and Etta settled in town and had three boys: Frederick, Louis, and Philip, all with the middle name of Noe. In Reverend Philip Noe Nelson's unpublished family history, he recounts his boyhood years at 676 St. George's Avenue, clearly remembering the endless winter job of caring for the furnace:

> . . . the house was heated by a pipeless coal furnace, the kind with a single large register in the floor of the living room. The furnace required attention 24 hours a day in Winter, with Mom stoking the furnace when Dad was at work. Each night the fire was "banked." In due time ashes had to be removed from the furnace, with Mom doing this task until one of us boys could do it safely. Then the ashes had to be taken to the back yard and put through a sieve to salvage any unburned pieces of coal. The ashes were scattered over the garden area, and the unburned coal returned to the cellar. It was a job none of us cherished, but if Dad told us to do it, it was done.

WOODBRIDGE SEAL. This symbol emphasizes the importance of clay to the economic development of the township.

By the late 1900s, immigrants from Poland, Austria, Hungary, and Italy also found their way here to work. Since many of the Hungarian men had served in the army of their country, they might arrive in America wearing their military uniforms, boots, short buttoned jackets, and jaunty hats decorated with feathers:

> Some of the new Hungarian immigrants coming as laborers to Woodbridge clay pits were housed in bunk houses, located on or near the clay area. A camp cook provided the meals and a sort of lumber camp atmosphere prevailed. Frequently, one or more of these miners would indulge themselves in a typical "old country" Hungarian treat known as "Solona." Having built a small wood fire, the miners impaled a hunk of fatback pork on a short, slender stick. The fatback was held over the fire and when the grease started to drip it was caught on a piece of sliced onion or tomato covered rye bread until saturation of the bread neared and then eaten with a gusto.[5]

The clay laborers worked long hours and struggled to feed large families on their meager wages. Often their only relaxation was a visit to a neighborhood tavern on payday to enjoy a few drinks with co-workers. Ruth Wolk remembered learning the words to a clay mining song in 1931 from Police Chief Patrick W.

Murphy. The many verses of "The Dreary Sand Hills" (the Fords section was often referred to as the Sand Hills because of its numerous clay and sand pits), usually composed on the spot, included the following lines:

> I came to Sand Hills to get me a job;
> I met Billy Barr, and he sent me to Bob,
> Saying if Bob doesn't give it, I'm sure Howe will
> Give you a job digging clay in the dreary Sand Hills.
>
> There is Francis Ostrander, who owns a clay mine,
> Pfeiffer, and Edgar, and Bob Valentine.
> If you don't get a job there, go down to Crows Mills,
> For its all the same clay on the dreary Sand Hills.
>
> But there is Tom Egan, who keeps the Bee Hive,
> He says I got whiskey to keep you alive.
> I got it this morning; it's fresh from the still,
> And the best to be had on the dreary Sand Hills.[6]

For years the township committee heard complaints from residents about the dangerous traveling conditions on the roads at night because companies were digging clay in the public highways. Finally, in 1869, the committee passed a law allowing clay miners and brick manufacturers to dig through roads to reach their clay banks on the opposite side as long as they provided "a good and sufficient road to accommodate the public travel. . . ." The complaints continued, however, as shown in the township committee's August 4, 1879 record, which ordered the overseer of Road District Number 28 to remove the obstructions in front of William Inslee's clay bank on the road leading from Woodbridge to Perth Amboy. Shortly after the close of the Civil War, a group of local owners and officers of clay companies formed a Clay Miners' Association. At a meeting held in 1866 at the Pike House, Charles M. Dally was elected president; Isaac Inslee, vice president; J. Mattison Melick, secretary; and Jacob R. Crossman, treasurer. A committee of three was organized to collect statistics about the Woodbridge clay industry and report at a future meeting. Undoubtedly these gentlemen discussed the deteriorating labor relations among the clay workers calling for higher wages.

Two strikes of clay laborers darkened the Woodbridge landscape during the late 1800s, strikes that mirrored the rising labor disputes in many growing American industries:

> After two postponements the clay miners of Woodbridge went out on strike on June 19th of 1866 and marched in a body from one clay mine to another forcing anyone willing to work to stop immediately. The protest deteriorated into a scene of violence when the miners, some armed with guns and clubs, mobbed the Township streets.

When the employers refused to yield to the demands of the employees, the strikers called a meeting for June 25th on the outskirts of the village to raise funds to maintain those who were destitute and also to bind themselves together for a three months' siege, if necessary. The appearance of the Sheriff with a posse of constables and special deputies broke up the meeting and the strikers fled into the nearby woods. After a day long chase, seven of the ringleaders were arrested and spent the night in the basement of the home of Samuel Dally on Main Street. By the middle of August, 1866, the strike was over and a majority returned to work at the old rates, whereupon to them the employers voluntarily increased the wages from $1.50 to $1.75 per day . . . (McElroy)

Another employee strike threatened in May 1873, but this time the Clay Miners' Association quickly resolved the situation.

In 1874, an estimated 265,000 tons of fire clay were dug annually in the vicinity and sent to market for use in many products such as sewer pipes, retorts, crucibles, facings for wallpaper, fine pottery and terra cotta ware, and firebrick. A ton of clay at the time sold for an average price of $3.50. In 1901, New Jersey was the largest producer of raw clay in the United States, but by 1920, the demand for the state's clays had begun a rapid decline. Clay had been discovered in Tennessee,

NANCY CHINA. A few examples of Nancy China's decorative ware exist today in private collections. (Ray J. Schneider)

Kentucky, Pennsylvania, Ohio, and other states that offered lower freight rates than New Jersey. Another reason for the slowdown involved the introduction of the continuous or car kiln, which replaced the periodic kiln for firing pottery. This change greatly slowed or stopped the use of saggers in the pottery trade. Saggers are containers or boxes made of fire-clay into which pottery is placed to protect it from flames during firing.

At the end of the 1800s, several New Jersey companies were manufacturing architectural terra cotta, a decorative, fire-resistant, cladding material. Terra cotta means "burnt earth" in Latin. The façade of the old Woodbridge National Bank on Main Street was constructed of terra cotta, and terra cotta seahorses are displayed on another Main Street building from the 1930s.

Nancy China, Inc. opened on upper Green Street in the 1940s and was probably the last pottery business to operate in town. Its products included sugar bowls, pitchers, covered boxes, and plates decorated with flower and fruit motifs. Rare examples of Nancy China exist today in the collections of Woodbridge residents.

According to Kreger's history:

> We should never lose sight of the fact that clay and/or sand is a "one time" crop. . . . Clay land, once it is removed from access to mining is lost forever to posterity . . . It would be fitting for our Town Fathers to erect somewhere in the area . . . a monument to Clay for all that it has meant to the Township of Woodbridge in its early, formative years.[7]

One symbol, however, endures as a reminder of the time when clay dominated the community's fortunes. The seal of Woodbridge Township includes a brick kiln, hand tools used for mining clay, and a ship's steering wheel. The emblem was originally designed in 1924 by Alfred J. Geiling of Fords for the dedication of the Memorial Municipal Building.

When interviewed in 1969, Geiling explained that he included the eagle to represent the United States, the miners' tools and kiln to symbolize the clay industry, and a gear to represent the coming of the machine age. In later designs, the gear became a ship's wheel representing the vessels that carried clay and bricks to market. A much earlier seal without any symbols was adopted by the township committee on November 11, 1885.

An intriguing postscript to the story of Woodbridge clay occurred in October and November 2001 at the site of the former Federal Terra Cotta Company on Cutter's Dock Road. While on an archeological dig on the property, members of the Historical Association of Woodbridge and the Cornelius Low House/Middlesex County Museum in Piscataway unearthed about 150 dummy terra cotta bombs from World War I.

A bomb weighs about 18.5 pounds each without its fins, nose, and tail plugs. "It looks like a slim football, almost 2 feet long with a maximum diameter of almost 6 inches. . . . The bombs, open at both ends, were used for training. They were filled with powdered plaster or flour and dropped from planes onto targets. A dummy bomb would explode on impact, leaving a large white spot."[8] Damaged during their original firing, these recently discovered artifacts are known as "wasters" and were discarded on the factory grounds.

TERRA COTTA BOMB WORKERS C. 1918. Local resident Severino Fiorentini stands third from left at the Federal Terra Cotta Company's factory, which produced dummy bombs during World War I. (Dr. Mario J. Fiorentini)

7. A MYRIAD OF MILESTONES: C. 1800–1930

Prior to 1800 the only roads used for travel through the Township were King George's Highway leading from the Raritan River at New Brunswick through Bonhamtown, the Sand Hills and Fords to Amboy Avenue at Main Street; a road from Perth Amboy now known as Amboy Avenue and St. George's Avenue to Newark . . . a road extending westerly from Rahway Avenue, now Green Street . . . and a road beginning at the mouth of Papiak [Woodbridge] Creek northwesterly through Sewaren and Port Reading to the Blazing Star Road near Rahway, now known as part of West Avenue and Old Road in Sewaren and Blair Road in Port Reading. —Leon McElroy

The post–Revolutionary War period saw great growth in travel and trade between New York and Philadelphia. With this increase came demands from private citizens and merchants in Woodbridge and throughout New Jersey for safer, smoother roads. In 1819, three armed men stopped the U.S. mail coach outside Rahway on the road to Elizabethtown. The masked bandits seized the horses, demanded the travelers' valuables, ransacked the mail, and disappeared. They were later caught in New York, tried, and sent to ten years of hard labor. In 1826, a similar hold-up occurred near Metuchen.

As these voices for change became more urgent, the concept arose that the people traveling on or benefiting from public roads should contribute to their construction, upkeep, and safety. Enter the toll road in New Jersey and the transition from local to centralized control of highways. Between 1801 and the advent of the railroad in the 1830s, an estimated 500 miles of turnpike roads were authorized in New Jersey.

On March 3, 1806, the Essex and Middlesex Turnpike Company was chartered. Several Rahway townsmen were among those authorized to obtain subscriptions to build a road 4 rods wide from the Raritan River to Newark. The charter provided that when 10 miles of road were finished, the governor would appoint three commissioners to check the workmanship. If all was well, he would issue a license to erect gates and turnpikes across the road "to demand and receive toll for each mile traveled." For every carriage or sleigh drawn by one "beast," the toll would be 1¢; four or more beasts would be 2¢. Milestones would be placed every mile from New Brunswick to Newark. There would be no tolls collected on

Sundays "from those passing to and fro to public worship." The road progressed through Metuchen, Uniontown (Iselin), Houghtonville (Colonia), Rahway, and Elizabeth to Newark.

The Perth Amboy Turnpike Company received permission in 1808 to construct a road from Perth Amboy to New Brunswick and then on to Easton, Pennsylvania. This road passed through Fords, the future Hopelawn and Raritan Township, and Metuchen. That same year the Woodbridge Turnpike Company ran its road over the Rahway River at William Edgar's landing to the stone bridge in Woodbridge "near the stores" (Heard's Square at Rahway Avenue and Green Street) then proceeding out Main Street to Fords and beyond. These turnpikes did not satisfy the desire of Woodbridge residents for new roads. In 1816, incorporators were permitted to collect subscriptions for 300 shares of stock at $25 a share to build a branch road from the Woodbridge Turnpike to the Arthur Kill. When 200 shares were sold, the men met at John Manning's Inn to give birth to the Woodbridge and Blazing Star Turnpike Company.

The War of 1812 was not on the agenda in Woodbridge until a special meeting of the township committee took place in May 1813. At that time the committee decided that residents should be assessed for defense against the enemy and voted $700 to the cause. It is not certain how the money was spent. Local men in the conflict most likely served with one of the volunteer companies from New Brunswick: Captain Nielson's Artillery, Captain VanDyke's Horse Artillery, Captain McKay's Riflemen, and Captain Scott's Light Infantry.

Although the peace treaty was signed in December 1814, news of the war's end did not reach Woodbridge until February 20, 1815. On that day townsfolk shot off

ROAD MARKER C. 1850. This milestone stood for years in Colonia on the northwest corner of Colonia Boulevard and New Dover Road on the Middlesex-Essex Turnpike.

a gun salute, tolled the church bells, and gathered in their houses of worship. Townspeople celebrated the peace again on March 2, 1815. Accompanied by a band from New Brunswick, residents marched in a procession to the First Presbyterian Church to hear addresses by several ministers and a reading of the Treaty of Peace. The group continued to a Major Osborne's house where everyone enjoyed roast ox hot off the spit. The gala day closed with a "National Salute" honoring the country. A newspaper of the time estimated that more than 3,000 people, many from neighboring counties, joined the festivities.

Townsfolk celebrated another historic moment on September 24, 1824, when Marquis de Lafayette, the famed Frenchman who aided the Americans during the Revolutionary War and was the last living major general of the conflict, stopped at the Cross Keys Tavern on his way to Philadelphia. Sixteen young ladies comprised his reception committee. Each wore a single letter fashioned of marigolds on the front of their white dresses, which together spelled "Welcome Lafayette."

Before the railroads came to town, freight and passenger services from the township to New York centered on water transportation. In 1821, the steamboat *Bridgetown Packet* sailed daily to the city from the Rahway River. By 1832, many vessels, including the *Tradesman, Nonpariel,* and *Lafayette,* gave Rahway travelers and merchants a wide choice, while several steamship lines docked at the New Blazing Star Landing on Staten Island Sound.

In 1844, the township committee authorized the construction of a dock at the mouth of Woodbridge Creek. The problems of opening a road to the dock, however, led the committee to abandon the project in favor of a wharf at Sewaren, which became known as Steamboat Dock. The *Thomas Hunt* sailing out of Perth Amboy in 1855 was probably the first steamboat to call at the new dock to pick up passengers heading for New York. In 1859, the *Iolas* plying between Keyport and New York City also called at Sewaren.

Until the close of the nineteenth century, many other steamboats circled from Keyport, New Brunswick, Perth Amboy, and Steamboat Dock to the city. Often one boat would replace an earlier vessel that had been destroyed by fire, found unsafe, or damaged by ice or in a fog. Their diverse names included *Mayflower, Neversink, Chicopee, Belle Horton,* and *William Harrison.* Sewaren residents always knew when the *General Sedgwick* was approaching, since the piercing sound of a steam calliope announced the boat's arrival all over the village. In 1864, the steamer *Sylvanshore* charged Sewaren passengers 20¢ for the New York run at a time when fares generally ran 25¢.

Area steamboat travelers braving endless delays caused by ice jams and fogs looked longingly to the train as a comfortable, speedy alternative. Petitions to the state legislature began in 1827 to permit railroads in New Jersey, and three years later bills were passed to establish the Camden-Amboy Railroad as well as a canal between the Delaware and Raritan Rivers. In 1832, the New Jersey Rail Road and Transportation Company (NJRR&T Co.) was authorized to construct the first railroad to serve the Woodbridge area. A stone bridge over the Rahway River opened the railroad into Rahway in October 1835. The following month a site for the Rahway depot was selected near Front Street, and a large hotel, the Mansion House, was built nearby. December 31, 1835 marked the trial run to Rahway with a locomotive pulling three baggage cars and four passenger cars carrying the railroad director and important guests.

Beneath a banner proclaiming "The People's Railroad," a huge crowd greeted the train's arrival. For the first three months, two steam trains and a horse-drawn train ran between Jersey City and Rahway for a fare of 62¢ one way. The engineers proudly announced that they could make the trip from Rahway to Newark in 30 to 34 minutes at the astonishing speed of 39 to 44 miles per hour. By 1853, ten trains made daily trips.

After two failed attempts to extend the railroad from Rahway to Perth Amboy, the branch through Woodbridge, which exists today, was authorized by the State in 1855. Shares of capital stock of the Perth Amboy and Woodbridge Railroad Company were offered at $20 each at the Pike House with Samuel Barron, James Valentine, and Adam Lee among the investors. The railroad finally opened nine years later.

When it first started, the NJRR&T Co. functioned as an individual company, which meant that passengers from Jersey City journeying to Trenton and Philadelphia had to make their own way across New Brunswick to board the Camden and Amboy Railroad. Travelers' stormy outcries finally persuaded the two railroads to merge their companies and tracks in 1867 and also combine with the Delaware and Raritan Canal Company to form the United Canal and Rail Road Companies of New Jersey or "Joint Companies," for short. In an attempt to stem competition from the Erie Canal and declining area freight rates, the Pennsylvania Railroad (PRR) obtained control of the Joint Companies in 1871 under a long lease. In this way the PRR acquired coveted railroad rights to New York City.

The Woodbridge Tramway Company was chartered in 1869 authorizing several Woodbridge and Perth Amboy investors in the clay industry to build trunk railroad lines in Middlesex County, which connected local clay mines, factories, and docks.

In 1873, John Taylor Johnston, president of the Central Railroad of New Jersey and a resident of Plainfield, purchased the Perth Amboy and Elizabethport Railroad. Work began the following year on the Sewaren station, the first depot to be constructed along the route of the railroad.

Charles Rolla, a C.W. Boynton Company employee, was struck by a train at the Main Street railroad crossing in 1874. This accident prompted the town to ask the railroad to place a flagman at the dangerous intersection. Two years later resident John Pfeiffer was hired as the first flagman at Main Street. The township committee later asked to extend the hours of the gatemen at Main and Green until 10 p.m. because of the many evening trains passing through town, and to place flagmen at the Berry and Freeman Street tracks. Gates were finally installed in 1886 at the Main and Green Street crossings, but even with gates and gatemen, accidents continued to happen.

CARTERET FERRY C. 1900. One of the many ferry boats plying the waters around Woodbridge in the days before the "Iron Horse" dominated transportation in the area.

Woodbridge had outgrown its railroad station by 1882 and requested the PRR to build a larger one. After the company sent a special trainload of officials to personally inspect the depot, the town donated land to provide landscaped entrances at Green and Pearl Streets. In August 1885, the new brick depot was at last ready, and ticket agent Charles Numbers moved into the apartment above the station.

Shortly before telegraph service was installed at the Woodbridge station, the flange on one of the driving wheels on an early morning train from New York broke loose and stalled the train. Since the conductor had no other way of reporting the problem, he hired a horse and carriage and drove to Rahway to arrange for another engine to push the train to Perth Amboy.

A fatal collision at the Green Street crossing on February 21, 1935, was especially disheartening to residents since the township committee had recently petitioned New Jersey to eliminate the town's grade crossings. A Shell Oil Company truck was struck by a PRR locomotive because the gates had not been closed. Although the truck exploded, its occupants were not hurt, but the gateman and engineer were killed. An investigation indicated that the gateman had failed to close the gates because he had suffered a stroke. At long last, the citizenry marked the end of the protracted grade crossing removal project with a massive parade, a host of visiting state and federal officials, including Secretary of the Navy Charles Edison, and a ribbon-cutting ceremony at the entrance of the new station on Pearl Street. Organized by Charles A. Gregory, editor of the *Independent-Leader*, the celebration on May 20, 1940 included a 19-gun salute by two field guns from the Raritan Arsenal to honor Secretary Edison, son of Thomas A. Edison.

The United States' War with Mexico (1846–1847) touched the lives of Woodbridge residents. Captain J. Mattison served as skipper of the U.S. brig *Bainbridge*, which carried Texas prisoners from Mexico to New Orleans in 1846, while several local men enlisted in the New Jersey Battalion for service in the brief conflict.

The election of Abraham Lincoln as president of the United States in 1860 brought Woodbridge face to face with the secession of Southern states, and the very real threat of a conflict fought on American soil. Lincoln carried every Northern state except New Jersey, where residents held strong opinions on both sides of the slavery question. In 1804, the state passed the controversial Gradual Abolition Act, which permitted New Jersey owners to free children born to slave mothers but required the children to serve the mother's master until age 21 if they were females, and 25, if males. Because of the complexities in the wording of this law, the freeing or manumission of slave children often did not take place. Abolitionist John Brown's raid on Harper's Ferry, Virginia, in 1859 disturbed citizens in Rahway, who called a mass meeting to publicly denounce the raid and express their outrage about the assault on the lives and property of the citizens of Virginia.

PRR STATION C. 1900. Ticket agent Charles Numbers lived above the Woodbridge station after it was completed in 1885.

Local Quakers assisted runaway slaves to escape to freedom in Canada on the Underground Railroad. The slaves followed secret routes by night from one safe place to another, guided by the stars. They crossed the Delaware River into New Jersey and continued on one of 12 routes with the Number One Route crossing Woodbridge Township. Guided by "conductors," who were often freed slaves themselves, the escapees moved by foot or horseback through Camden, Burlington, Bordentown, and Princeton to New Brunswick where they frequently met opposition when trying to cross the Raritan River.

President Lincoln declared war when Confederate soldiers fired on Fort Sumter in Charleston, South Carolina, on April 12, 1861. Fifty-one town residents answered the first call to arms later that year. Several men, members of the recently formed Pike Guard, joined with the Clark Guard of Rahway to form Company "H" of the 5th New Jersey Volunteer Infantry. They signed on in Trenton for three years. The company later joined with the 6th, 7th, and 8th New Jersey Volunteer Infantries, which formed the Third Brigade of General Joseph "Fighting Joe" Hooker's Division of the Third Army Corps.

Two months after the war started, Southern sympathizers in Rahway hung an effigy of President Lincoln high on a liberty pole at Scudders School House. Other residents were outraged, especially when they found that the pole was greased and had to be chopped down to rescue "Mr. Lincoln." Phineas F. Frazee of Rahway was arrested in August for offering a captain's commission in the Confederate Army to another resident, Joseph Gabriel. Frazee was later set free because he had not persuaded Gabriel to enlist.

The Third Brigade suffered great losses when they followed the rebels to Williamsburg, Virginia, to fight a bloody battle on May 5, 1862. Five hundred men of Hooker's Division were wounded, killed, or listed as missing after a torturous battle waged in drenching rain and deep mud.

Woodbridge was especially saddened by the death of 24-year-old Lieutenant William C. Berry, who was shot in the heart at the Battle of Williamsburg, his first engagement. Son of the clay magnate William H. Berry, young William attended Strawberry Hill School and Woodbridge Hall, a private school in Perth Amboy. While recovering at 16 from a long illness, he helped his father in his farming and manufacturing businesses, and in 1859 he invented a root cutter for chopping cattle feed, a tool that brought him a citation from the New Jersey Agricultural Society. Before the war he worked as engineering superintendent in his father's factory and had made plans to market his root cutter. Berry joined the Pike Guard as a drillmaster and later was commissioned a lieutenant in Company "H."

Lieutenant Berry's body was brought back to Woodbridge by train and amid banners of mourning crepe was escorted through town by members of the Pike Guard with their firearms held in reverse. Soldiers maintained a watch over his body, which lay in state at the Methodist Church until his military funeral was held on May 24, 1862, at the First Presbyterian Church. Berry was interred at the Methodist church's cemetery. His remains were moved at a later time to the Alpine Cemetery in Perth Amboy.

CIVIL WAR VETERAN. Private Samuel Coddington served in Company H of the 5th New Jersey Volunteer Infantry from August 1861 to December 1863, when he was discharged on disability. He later became Woodbridge postmaster. (George Ryan)

Several other township servicemen from Company "H" were killed, wounded, or listed as missing after the Battle of Williamsburg. Local soldiers commended for courage and gallantry included Sergeants John W. Flanigan and Frederick Brill, Corporals Lewis F. Noe and John Sutton, and Privates Charles C. and George W. Dally, Patrick Kane, and Dallas Noe. After Williamsburg, Company "H" took part in several skirmishes and attacks in Virginia. Later in 1862, they crossed the Rappahannock River on pontoons under continual Confederate fire and camped at Fredericksburg. They did not see action again until the following May when they engaged in an assault with fixed bayonets at St. Mary's Heights. Woodbridge soldiers also fought at Chancellorsville, Virginia, in 1863.

About twelve town men served in the U.S. Navy during the war, of whom Thomas McElroy was the most well known. After various assignments he was ordered to duty on the ironclad *Mound City*, a wooden ship with iron armor plating. McElroy shot down a large Confederate flag from the flagstaff at Fort St. Charles on the White River in Virginia and sent the flag back home to Woodbridge in June 1862. When residents flew the flag from the Pike House flagpole, an unidentified patriot hoisted the Stars and Stripes above the Confederate flag. Shortly thereafter the Confederates blew up the *Mound City*, leaving McElroy and the ship's surgeon as the only survivors.

The surrender of General Robert E. Lee at Appomattox on April 9, 1865, brought much rejoicing to Woodbridge citizens, but their happiness was cut short by the shocking news of President Lincoln's assassination. The funeral train bearing Lincoln's body stopped briefly at the Rahway station on April 24 to allow local mourners to glimpse the casket through the train windows.

As the agonies of the Civil War faded through the years, Woodbridge turned its attention to peacetime enterprises. These endeavors represented the needs and interests of an established, contemporary community with a diverse and expanding population. (The growth of schools and churches is covered in the next two chapters.)

In 1875, Woodbridge native Thomas Barron left $50,000 in his will to build a free public library in town. While working in his father's store at the age of 14, Thomas Barron developed a keen sense for business transactions and later amassed a fortune from the trading house he established to deal in the West Indies. After retirement, Barron lived in New York City and devoted his time to philanthropy, historical research, and fishing. "Few men were better read, and few men were better able to arrange and utilize their mental acquisitions."[1]

Thomas's nephew Dr. John C. Barron, a surgeon with the U.S. Army during the Civil War and executor of his uncle's will, donated land for the library on Rahway Avenue, which was part of the original Barron homestead. The Barron Library, the first free public library in Middlesex County, opened on September 11, 1877.

An architectural gem, the Barron Library was built in Romanesque Revival style with many intricate architectural details including an arched ceiling, clock tower, stained-glass windows, and tiled floors. Architect J. Cleveland Cady also designed the facade of the original Metropolitan Opera House in New York City. A fireplace decorated with 65 blue-and-white Delft tiles from Holland, each

BARRON ARTS CENTER, C. 1900. Formerly the Barron Free Public Library, this stately landmark stands on Rahway Avenue at Port Reading Avenue

depicting a Biblical scene, highlights the reception room, while a beautiful rose window measuring 5 feet in diameter illuminates the gallery. The library was placed on the State and National Registers of Historical Places in 1977, the only property in the township to be listed. Today the building houses the Barron Arts Center, which is dedicated to bringing art exhibits, musical programs, lectures, art classes, displays of local history, poetry readings, and other cultural programs to the township.

Woodbridge's weekly newspaper, the *Independent Hour*, issued its first copy on Thursday, April 13, 1876. A yearly subscription cost $2. Another local paper, the *Leader-Journal*, followed some years later. In 1919, Maxwell Logan started the *Independent*, which competed with the *Leader-Journal* until 1939, when the papers joined forces under the combined title, the *Independent-Leader*, with Hugh Williamson Kelly as president and Charles E. Gregory as managing editor. The paper ceased publication in 1965.

In 1893, John Thompson, postmaster and owner of a harness shop, proposed to the township committee that a hook and ladder be purchased for the town. Four years later, the Woodbridge Fire Company was organized as a volunteer unit and added a hose cart, 400 feet of hose, and a dozen fire buckets. Charles R. Brown served as the first president of the Board of Fire Commissioners from 1897 to 1939 and was succeeded by Leon E. McElroy.

Carpenter's Livery Stable on Pearl Street supplied two fondly remembered teams of horses to the fire company. Stories circulated for years about "Tom" and "Harry," horses that could not wait to gallop to the firehouse on School Street whenever they heard the alarm. The pair stood ready to be harnessed to the fire wagon and then raced off to put out the fire. "Buddie" and "Buster" followed in their hoof steps and worked until 1922, when, in an ironic twist of fate, they were killed in a fire that destroyed Carpenter's Stable. After the horses died, the men pulled the fire wagon by hand or commandeered any team of horses driving by at their time of need. While separate fire companies operated in the various local sub-divisions, the Woodbridge Police Force served the entire township.

Patrick "Big Paddy" Cullinane became Woodbridge's first policeman. He was named constable in 1895 and an officer the following year. Cullinane was a larger-than-life figure about town: tall of stature and presumably with such large hands that he could lift a suspect by the collar and transport him single-handedly to the lockup. The duties of the police at this time centered on keeping tramps out of town, dispelling crowds congregating on street corners, and catching unlicensed dogs. Early policemen received $40 a month for their services.

In 1911, Woodbridge organized an official police force after legislation was passed by the state that authorized higher pay, uniforms, and a merit system for salaries and promotions. Patrick Murphy was named chief, with Patrick Cullinane, Michael McDonald, Hans Simonsen, and James Walsh comprising the force. Police duties increased as the immigrant population grew in town. Many of the clay and brick workers knew little English and often violated laws that they did not understand. Until police cars came into general use, transporting offenders

CARPENTER'S LIVERY STABLE C. 1915. Located on the corner of Main and Pearl Streets, the stable housed the two famous horse teams that pulled the first Woodbridge Fire Company wagon. (Rev. Philip N. Nelson)

from outlying sections to the police station on Main Street was often a challenge. A patrolman might have to ride on one or more trolleys with a recalcitrant offender in tow who had only one thought in mind—to make a getaway.

In 1935, the first police radio system was installed in town, a state-of-the-art innovation at the time. A new police headquarters opened next to the town hall in 1964, and the following year a Police Cadet Training Program, the first in New Jersey, was initiated to provide trained patrolmen.

That man of many talents, C.W. Boynton, can probably be credited with introducing an early form of mass transit. He appeared before the township committee in 1893 to obtain a right-of-way for the first electric railway (trolley) in Woodbridge. The 17-mile line, known as the Woodbridge and Sewaren Electric Street Railway Company, ran from Rahway to Boynton Beach in Sewaren. Service started two years later, following a route along Rahway Avenue, Woodbridge-Sewaren Road, and East Avenue. Also in 1893, plans were formulated in Perth Amboy to extend the Railroad Avenue (State Street) Trolley Line to Woodbridge Creek. The city carried the line to the creek, but the bridge never materialized. Passengers heading to and from Perth Amboy were transported across the creek on a unique ferryboat with neither sails nor engine. The boat was pulled from bank to bank by a chain that ran through the ferry over an idler pulley. A primitive conveyance at best, the ferry consisted of a wooden platform built on a barge covered with a flat roof and surrounded by a picket fence to keep passengers out of the creek.

Two trolley lines operated by the Raritan Traction Company ran through parts of town. One line rolled along through Perth Amboy to Keasbey, Fords, and New Brunswick, while another ran from Perth Amboy through Sewaren, Woodbridge, and Avenel to Newark. Opinions pro and con flared over a proposed trolley to Carteret, and another through Woodbridge proper, while folks in Fords complained that the fare from Fords Corner to Perth Amboy should be five cents instead of a dime. Ultimately the whole trolley industry became moot when the Public Service Transportation Company took over the Rahway and Perth Amboy lines in the 1920s, tore up the tracks, and replaced the trolleys with busses.

Two venerable organizations, Americus Lodge Number 83 of the Free and Accepted Masons; and the Salmagundi Musical and Literary Society, organized after the Civil War. The Masons incorporated in 1867, meeting first at the old Masonic Hall, and after 1928, at the Craftsman's Club, both on Green Street. The clubhouse was actually built around an existing home that originally belonged to the Brewster family. When the membership dwindled in the 1960s, the remaining Masons joined the Perth Amboy organization. Local couples formed the Salmagundi Society in 1882 and prepared papers on timely topics for presentation at evening meetings. The society, which continued into the 1960s, held an annual, formal-dress Guest Night, which often took place at the home of Edith and Hampton Cutter on Green Street.

The township of Woodbridge also lost some of its original land during the late nineteenth and early twentieth centuries. The state legislature created the County of Union in 1860, which removed lower Rahway (Leesville) and Milton from Woodbridge and Middlesex County. Ten years later, the state established Raritan (now Edison) Township in Middlesex County, which included part of Piscataway Township and the Metuchen section of Woodbridge. In 1906, the state incorporated the Borough of Roosevelt (Carteret) against the wishes of the Woodbridge government, who feared tax inequities. The Court of Common Pleas appointed three commissioners to divide the assets and liabilities between Roosevelt and Woodbridge.

Roosevelt ultimately paid for some sewer assessments, and according to Ruth Wolk, "got the best of the deal." Because the name Carteret continued to be used by many people, Roosevelt became Carteret again in 1922. The village of Chrome, located within the boundaries of Carteret, was named for the Chrome Steel Works, a factory originally from Brooklyn, New York. The company, which "took its name from chrome steel produced by adding chromium to the furnace charge," built a large steel mill in Carteret between 1902 and 1904.[2] A U.S. post office also opened in Chrome in 1904 and closed on August 31, 1922, to reopen the next day as the Roosevelt Post Office, which itself ended service three months later. After that time, all mail was handled by the Carteret Post Office.

War came again to Woodbridge, briefly this time, when the Spanish downed the battleship *Maine* in 1898. Nine local residents are believed to have served in the Spanish-American War, which ended later that year.

Main Street was transforming itself from a country road with scattered stores into a downtown shopping district. Brothers Chris and John "Pete" Christensen, tailors from Denmark, opened their department store on the north side of Main Street in 1895. Christensen's moved across the street in 1933, where the store continued until the family closed the business and sold the building in June 1998. New Yorker Morris Choper opened his department store on Main Street in 1915, aided by his wife Lena. Interviewed in 1964 by the *Independent-Leader*, Choper recalled that there were no lights on Main Street in 1915, the street was unpaved, and "it was a constant pull to make a living." Speaking of local stores of that time, Choper remembered Drake's Drug Store, Rich and John Neary's Butcher Shops, Blum's Market, Kath's Grocery, Ostrowich's Shoe Store, and Christensen's, the oldest existing store.

As Woodbridge and the surrounding region moved from an agricultural to an industrial economy during the later years of the nineteenth century, the need for a dependable water supply became a necessity. The Middlesex Water Company, "one of the largest investor-owned water utilities in New Jersey and one of the most successful," was organized in 1897 and continues today to supply safe water to a large area of central New Jersey.[3] By the 1980s the company had long outgrown its corporate offices at 52 Main Street at the corner of Pearl Street. Middlesex Water had moved into the familiar Woodbridge National Bank

Clang! Clang! Clang! c. 1895. C.W. Boynton introduced the trolley to the township to entice day trippers to his resort in Sewaren.

building in the 1930s after the bank closed its doors during the Depression. (The building today houses the Woodbridge Chamber of Commerce.) Construction started in 1981 for a new company headquarters and maintenance complex on Ronson Road in Iselin. In 1984, two brick-and-glass buildings opened, providing office space and a large garage and shop to maintain the company's fleet of trucks.

The years between 1800 and the early 1930s saw Woodbridge transformed from an agricultural settlement to an industrial center dominated by the huge clay industry. The population expanded and diversified, community services and schools organized, and water and rail transportation and safer, paved streets and highways took the place of horses and wagons on dusty roads. The township, along with the rest of the country, emerged from the Civil War with broader views on domestic and economic issues. Residents could look back on the many milestones of change they encountered in the nineteenth century, milestones that would lead them into an enormously transformed twentieth-century worldview.

ALL ABOARD! Without sails or engine, this unusual conveyance carried passengers for 2¢ each way between Sewaren and Perth Amboy c. 1890.

8. EDUCATION ON THE MOVE: c. 1789 ONWARD

Tis education forms the common mind: Just as the twig is bent the tree's inclined. —
Alexander Pope (from *Moral Essays I*)

After years of discussion and dissention, the township government voted in 1789
to authorize the use of the interest from the School Fund and the dog tax revenue
to pay for "the schooling of poor people's children." This arrangement lasted until
1825, when the committee diverted the dog taxes to pay for damages caused by
wandering sheep. Apparently, Woodbridge had not yet gotten those wooly
creatures under control since the days when the Sheep Common was first set
aside for them.

Jonathan Freeman, known for his Revolutionary War intelligence activities,
built Woodbridge Academy on the west side of Rahway Avenue in 1794 for
approximately $1,650. The academy was home to several private school ventures
through the years. In 1829, it was known as the Woodbridge Classical and
Commercial Institute, offering preparatory courses for college, West Point
Military Academy, and "the Navy." Through the years, many town fathers,
including members of the Cutter, Bloomfield, Freeman, Potter, and Brown
families, became subscribers of the school.

One of the first champions of public school education in New Jersey,
Middlesex County assemblyman James Parker of Perth Amboy (a cousin of James
Parker, the printer) initiated legislation to establish a state fund for free schools in
1817. In 1829, Woodbridge voted to raise $400 through taxes to be added to its
allotted state allowance for education.

A private high school known as Woodbridge Seminary, Elm Tree Institute, and
later as Morris Academy opened in 1826 under the direction of James Stryker on
the site of Henry Potter's Inn on Rahway Avenue. The rigorous curriculum
included Latin, Greek, Hebrew, English, French, Spanish, chemistry, history, and
botany, as well as bookkeeping, algebra, and "geometry with practical application
to surveying." In 1843, the trustees of the academy faced a teacher problem. The
academy minutes read, "Resolved that Thomas H. Morris is teacher downstairs.
Resolved that Anna Mariah Stansbee is teacher upstairs for 3 months, subject to
withdrawal at the expiration of that time if necessary to have a male teacher." Poor

Miss Stansbee did lose her job because the trustees believed she had failed as a disciplinarian. The trustees decided that a new building should replace the old academy and began construction in 1849. The following year Isaac Inslee purchased the original schoolhouse for $70 and moved it closer to the intersection with Green Street, where it later housed the *Independent Hour*.

Several private schools opened in the Rahway area during the early nineteenth century. They included a military academy, an evening school known as Lee's Ville Academy, the Athenian Academy, and the Rahway Seminary under the direction of a Mr. and Mrs. Burnham. The seminary charged $150 a year for board and tuition with $10 extra for instruction in instrumental music and another $5 to practice the piano. Several Rahway citizens met at the home of Jacob R. Shotwell in 1848 to "incorporate the trustees of the Rahway School for colored children." In 1863, shortly after Rahway separated from Woodbridge Township, the legislature passed a law allowing funds for the school to continue under the supervision of the Society of Friends.

The New Jersey School Act of 1846 allowed school districts to incorporate by adopting a name and a seal and recording the boundaries of the district with the county clerk. By incorporating, a district could raise taxes by a two-third vote for a school building and maintenance. About this time male teachers in Woodbridge were paid $375 a year and female teachers received $180 per annum. Equal pay for equal work was a concept whose time had not yet arrived.

In 1851, the Strawberry Hill School trustees planted shade trees around the schoolhouse and dug a spring to supply drinking water. No longer would the pupils have the excuse of leaving their lessons to get a cup of water at a neighboring house. But by 1860, the board had sold the school and purchased property from William Harned for a new school on the south side of Main Street near the future Columbus Avenue. The Strawberry Hill and Jefferson districts were consolidated, with the new school taking the name of Jefferson. (It is not known whether there was an original Jefferson School.)

Jefferson School opened in March 1866 but closed its doors later that year, suffering from a lack of funds. Neighbors were puzzled on December 13, 1866, when they saw the schoolhouse flag flying upside down at half staff. Principal Hays announced to the gathering crowd that he and his scholars were protesting their lack of a suitable stove to heat the schoolroom. The trustees quickly purchased a new stove, but financial woes continued to plague the school, which closed again the following April.

In May six taxpayers voted to raise $500 to reopen Jefferson and also agreed to hire an assistant to help the teacher instruct her 105 students! Jefferson students were known as the "uptowners," while academy pupils were the "downtowners," with a running discussion and friendly rivalry continuing between the schools to determine which was "superior."

The eternal problem of finances caused the Jefferson trustees to try to dismiss the principal, J. Ward Smith, in 1871, and hire a woman to replace him, presumably at a lower salary. Smith, however, was undeterred. He informed the trustees that he was hired for the entire school year and would not be leaving before that time. Mr. Smith completed his contract.

The school districts consolidated in 1871, and a single board assumed the operation of all local public schools. Plans were also started for School Number One, which would serve as Woodbridge's flagship school for years to come. On October 11, 1875, residents packed the Masonic Hall to discuss the proposal. By January 21 of the following year, clay manufacturer William H. Berry reported that the trustees would purchase property from James Valentine on a proposed new street, first known as Brown Street, then Central Avenue, and finally School Street. The trustees made a motion that the building should not exceed $25,000, a figure that caused a lengthy, heated debate but finally passed. Work progressed swiftly, and on July 7, 1876, the trustees named Harry Anderson as the first principal at $100 per month; Sarah E. Eldridge, vice principal at $600 for the 11-month school year; and Kate A. Moore, teacher, at $400 for the year.

The board purchased an impressive clock for $600 and a proper school bell weighing 1,500 pounds for the tower. McElroy reported that the clockworks "were placed 35 feet from the dials which were 6 feet in length and which prevented the works from being affected by the shaking of the tower when the bell was being rung. The striking apparatus of the clock was operated through a hammer, which struck upon the outside of the bell." The bell was inscribed, "School District #24, A.D, 1876. C.W. Boynton, President, Howard Valentine,

NEW ROLE FOR SCHOOL C. 1944. After moving to the corner of Main and Pearl, the old Jefferson School relocated further down Main to become an auto supply store and gas station. Note the service flag with two stars in the upper left window. (Tara Dubay)

D.C. [*district clerk*], William H. Berry and Charles Campbell, Trustees. Wisdom is better than gold."

All was ready for a grand opening on January 6, 1877. Woodbridge clergymen conducted the dedication, and Howard Valentine presented the keys to Principal Anderson, who promptly told the audience that there was a deficit of $60 in the building budget. In his speech, Berry explained that $2,300 more was needed to complete the building, but apparently these monetary worries did not dim the enthusiasm of the day.

Shortly after opening, parents complained at a crowded meeting that the ventilation of the sanitary facilities was inadequate and also questioned the purity of the drinking water from a well close to the outdoor bathrooms. Berry admitted that the ventilation was poor and suggested that townsfolk take a drink from the well and decide for themselves about the water. No one found fault with it, but Boynton suggested that the board obtain the opinion of "scientific men." The problems were tabled for the future.

Since students supplied their own textbooks at this time, teachers often suggested favorite stores or encouraged them to purchase texts from friends of the instructors. When this situation reached the trustees, they ruled that students could buy books at any store that sold them, including the local establishments of Commoss and Ensign, C. Drake, M.A. Brown, and Mrs. Luckhurst.

After School One was up and running, the Jefferson School closed permanently. The schoolhouse was moved about 1877 to a corner of Main and

SCHOOL ONE. Now an enduring landmark, School One stood in open country when it was built in 1877.

Pearl Streets to become a feed store and later moved again to a site across from the Town Hall.

Several "firsts" took place at School One in 1881. Joseph H.T. Martin presented $20 to the trustees to be divided among the top students in each classroom, the first prizes to be awarded for scholarship. Later that year Miss M.J. Thomas, principal at the time, suggested the first report card for the intermediate department. She wanted parents to be notified monthly about the deportment of their children. Woodbridge High School, which was part of School One, graduated its first class. Students Sidney Pearson, Sadie Brewster, Clara Melick, and Lulu Bloodgood received certificates of graduation for completing a three-year course of study.

The quality of the teaching staff appeared on the trustees' agenda in 1883. After a lengthy discourse, they decided that after September 1, 1884, instructors must have some normal school training in the methods of teaching. (Normal schools offered a two-year curriculum providing high school graduates with teaching certificates.)

Previously, an ambitious young woman "finishing her readers" would be qualified to teach without further study. Several teachers took leaves of absence to complete their credentials. In 1887, the forward-looking Miss Thomas presented a plan to divide the high school courses from the grammar grades' curriculum. She proposed high school studies in algebra, philosophy, geography, history, chemistry, rhetoric, English literature, and composition.

The question of teachers from town versus teachers from out of town confounded the board in April 1889. Several trustees believed that teachers residing in town should be given preference when jobs opened up, but Boynton believed the board should look outside of Woodbridge for qualified instructors. Either way, the trustees had difficulty locating teachers since the applicants were requesting larger salaries than the board was willing to pay. Later that year, this advertisement appeared in the *New York World*: "Teacher Wanted in graded school in a village in New Jersey. Salary $350 a year. Must be normal graduate. Address with recommendations. Teacher Box 343, World Office, New York." The board received several responses, all but one were from male teachers, and apparently the trustees were looking for women to whom they could pay lower salaries. They inserted the ad a second time with the salary raised to $375, but again they were not pleased with the candidates. Finally A.H. Wilson, the current principal, was dispatched to New York City to personally unearth suitable instructors. Just in time for the first day of school, he hired Miss Inez J. Hallock.

The thorny educational issues of the day were put aside on July 4, 1890, when School One marked a rousing, patriotic occasion. The estate of Jotham Coddington, a descendent of a colonial family, had bequeathed a giant white oak tree to the school for a flagpole. After the tree was cut and contributions collected for the flag, the school was ready for a flag-raising ceremony and parade. School officials purchased two flags, one for parades and state occasions and an 18-foot flag to be raised and lowered each school day.

WHS FACULTY, 1924. Left to right (bottom row): L.W. Woodman, Anne Caster, Charles H. Boehm; (second row) M.J. McElroy, Sara C. FitzGerald, Marguerite D. Miller, Edith W. White, Bryan C. Rothfuss; (third row) Isaac H. Gilhuly, Edna Welsh, Marie B. Dunigan, Frances C. Shults, Seymour R. Willits; (top row) Ethel A. Inslee, Mrs. F.P. Edgar, Grace Huber, Margaret C. Crampton, Violet G. Lippincott, and Anna C. Frazer.

When 113 students came down with measles in October 1890, the board closed School One for a short time. Two years later, diphtheria took the lives of several children and caused the school to close for over a month. While the building was empty, the trustees ordered the washing of desks and woodwork with a solution of bichloride of mercury and the rooms and outer buildings fumigated with burning sulphur. Workers destroyed drinking cups, slates, and lead pencils, and cleaned and refilled the fire buckets that hung in the halls. The diphtheria epidemic also resolved the earlier concern about the school's well water. The old well was now filled in and a new one dug on the other side of the building.

Memorial Day 1893 was an especially memorable jubilee for the school after the dread diphtheria epidemic had run its course. Grand Army of the Republic veterans led the line of march in a parade on Main Street. They were followed by the students and civic organizations. Carrying large flags and bouquets for the soldiers' graves, the pupils gathered at Trinity Episcopal Church cemetery to sing patriotic songs and hear student Willie Voorhees give a speech honoring the country's war dead. School records reported that "The marching and behavior of the children were excellent and no doubt impressions were made upon their minds that will bring forth a high order of patriotic devotion in the future."[1]

In 1894, a new state school law abolished the trustees as overseers of individual schools and introduced boards of education to administer to all public schools in a town or city. Candidates from all corners of town threw their hats into the ring to serve on the first official nine-member Woodbridge Township Board of Education. C.W. Boynton, John Correja Jr., Charles B. Demarest, John H. Hilsdorf, Joshua Liddle, John Lockwood, Joseph W. Savage, C.B. Smith, and Howard Valentine won the prized seats. School One, Blazing Star #2, Rahway Neck #3, Washington #4, Locust Grove #5, Iselin #6, Fairfield #7, and Keasbey #8 were now supervised by the new board. In 1894, 1,278 students attended the township schools, with 794 of them enrolled at School One.

The board quickly realized that with consolidation came larger expenditures. No longer could pencils and pen holders be bought by the dozen; now they were ordered by the gross and black ink in 5-gallon bottles. The members faced many difficult decisions, which included problems with principals, a new Keasbey school, building repairs, truancy, discipline, and teachers' salaries. No matter of economics was too trifling, as evidenced by this 1895 resolution: "It was moved and carried that the clerk request the janitor of No. 1 School to light the lamp in front of the school house, only on evenings when the moon is not shining."

The following year, the well-respected and innovative John Henry Love took the reins as principal of School One and immediately strengthened the high school curriculum. He ordered equipment for a chemistry lab and introduced new English and Latin courses. Three teachers now comprised the high school faculty: Mr. Love himself and the Misses Mary Van Arsdale and Albarata Dilks. In 1897, Love's salary was raised from $1,200 to $1,400 a year. That same year he persuaded the board to install bicycle racks in the basement of the school to accommodate the many students from outlying areas who biked to classes. Resident J. Blanchard Edgar came before the board in 1898 to request that the standards of School One be raised so that it would offer an education equal to the schools in Perth Amboy and Rahway. Moved by Mr. Edgar's plea, the board immediately instructed the textbook committee to purchase those books that would uplift the school's objectives.

The closing year of the century saw the board turn down a new school for Sewaren because students could easily ride the new trolley to Woodbridge, and they voted to build one in Port Reading. During that summer, Love was promoted to supervising principal of the schools. In 1900, the board set aside funds to transport students from Carteret to the high school at School One. This first appropriation toward the bussing of district students marked the beginning of a major school budget item from that time forward to the present day.

Dissention arose when Carteret (Roosevelt) seceded in 1906, taking with it a recently completed school financed by Woodbridge, but Carteret finally agreed to pay off the outstanding bonds. Teachers' salaries that year ranged from $450 to $800. By 1909, the problem of overcrowded schools had reached the tipping point, and immediate action was necessary. The board moved classes from School One to the Hungarian Parish House next door and to the firehouse across the street to relieve overcrowding, but the members understood that a separate high school was an absolute necessity.

MR. LOVE BUYS A CAR!

Supervising Principal John H. Love was among the first Woodbridge residents to purchase an automobile. In the fall of 1909, the board of education voted to pay for the gasoline used while Mr. Love was traveling on school business. No information on the make and model seem to exist, but the motor was located in the rear of the car.

A furor arose about the estimated amount of $70,000 for the proposed high school, but the legal voters in the district approved the budget with 128 yeas to 88 nays. Since about 30 people usually voted in school elections, this turn-out was record-breaking. New Jersey Governor J. Franklin Fort laid the cornerstone on Barron Avenue on October 6, 1910, and Woodbridge High School (WHS) officially opened in 1911. The school continued as the only high school until 1956.

The early years of the twentieth century saw many additions to the educational programs, especially at the high school: a night vocational school in 1915, military training in 1916 (added because of the impending war with Germany), compulsory physical education in 1917, and domestic arts, manual training, and

HAIRBOWS AND HIGH BUTTON SHOES. These School One pupils posed in front of their building c. 1910.

EARLY SCHOOL, C. 1844. Woodbridge Academy, a semi-private school, is located in the left foreground of this wood engraving of Rahway Avenue.

music in 1919. The first school nurse also arrived in 1919, as well as the introduction of summer school programs. At the request of Frank Valentine, German language instruction was dropped from the curriculum in April 1918. Upcoming seniors were permitted to finish their German studies, and some time after the Armistice, German was reinstated.

Extracurricular activities at WHS were also expanding. Miss Anna C. Frazer directed the orchestra and glee club, started about 1916, while the first band took to the field in 1926. Debating was popular with rousing, interscholastic competitions complete with cheerleaders and special songs. Baseball, the first organized school sport, began back in 1899, when the high school was part of School One. The team enjoyed a championship season in 1925, and another successful year in 1934, when the WHS Red Ghosts closed their season by shutting out South River High, a powerhouse team that had not been defeated in 29 consecutive games.

New classrooms, offices, an auditorium, an annex, and new wings were added through the years to accommodate the burgeoning high school population, but no amount of expansion could prevent the initiation of a "temporary" double session starting in September 1933. Freshmen and some sophomores attended the afternoon session; all other students arrived early and were dismissed at noon. The elementary schools also scheduled double sessions at this time.

Woodbridge faculty members have been affiliated with teachers' unions for many years. Educators joined the American Federation of Teachers in 1945 as Local 822 with WHS faculty member Stephen K. Werlock as the first president.

By the 1950s, the majority of teachers belonged to the Woodbridge Township Federation of Teachers (WTFT), with the Woodbridge Township Education Association (WTEA), an affiliate of the National Education Association, representing a smaller number. For years a rivalry existed between the two unions with competing musical programs presented annually by each group. In 1967, the WTFT called for a strike that lasted 11 days and centered on wages and other issues. The second and last strike within the district took place in 1978.

In 1976 and 1981, the WTEA challenged the leadership of the WTFT, but lost both elections. In 1983, however, the WTEA was successful and has solely represented Woodbridge teachers since that time. Today the WTEA also includes educational support staff employees with a total membership of 1,600. Toyce Collins, a former teacher, has served as full-time president of the WTEA, which maintains an office at 34 Green Street.

Unfortunately, the building of a new Woodbridge High School on Samuel Lupo Drive (formerly Kelly Street) in 1956 was short of space also, and the double session continued there until 1964. Old WHS became a junior high in 1956 with three new junior high schools in Fords, Iselin, and Colonia opening in 1959–1960. Students first entered John F. Kennedy Memorial High School in Iselin and Avenel Junior High in September 1964.

The seemingly never-ending saga of the Free School lands in Iselin reached a final determination in 1966 with the help of the New Jersey Supreme Court. For years the property served as the Woodbridge "Poor Farm," where the destitute and those serving sentences on municipal charges worked to pay for their support with any yearly profit paid to the board of education. This arrangement ended in 1920 when Woodbridge acquired a poor house in Port Reading. Private farming continued on the Iselin land until the early 1950s, when the trustees sold off the top soil. Except for the tri-annual election of the seven-member board of trustees, the property was forgotten and neglected for many years. Since traditionally women served as trustees, they were nicknamed the "Seven Sisters."

The State of New Jersey received 30 acres of the School Lands in 1949 as part of the right-of-way for the Garden State Parkway. After the parkway opened in 1951, the remaining land became attractive commercial property. Four years later, the trustees signed a contract to sell most of the acreage to a manufacturing company for $275,000. As soon as this proposal was announced, Arnold Graham, a certified public accountant and municipal chairperson of the local Republican Party, brought a citizen's suit against the township. Graham charged that the sale was illegal and the price far too low. All public entities involved with the Free School Lands through the years were included in the action, but the Supreme Court ultimately ruled that only the trustees, the board of education, and the township committee held legal interest in the property. In July 1961, these groups agreed to collaborate on the best use of the land. With Mayor Frederick M. Adams representing the majority view, six township committee members voted in favor and four opposed retaining the land as a town-owned industrial park. During the next several years, the officials continued discussions about the Free School

Lands. The property was auctioned to the highest bidder, Paley, Tucker & Green, of Perth Amboy, who paid $932,000 for the 130-acre tract. The profit from the sale would be used to upgrade the Woodbridge School System while future tax revenue would be placed in the treasury. The Computer Center of Eastern Airlines opened in 1968 as the first building of the Parkway Industrial Center. Siemens America Inc., Sutton Construction Company, and Prudential Insurance followed. Iselin historians Tex Perry and David Miller noted this development as follows:

> So ends the public's use of the Iselin "free school" lands. The citizens have benefitted by its existence in varying degree over the past 300 years and [to] a far greater extent than initially contemplated by Governor Phillip Carteret when providing for its creation in 1669, as a source of income for the parochial school of the established religion.[3]

The 93-year-old bell tower of School One was removed in 1967 because of the safety hazard presented by its decaying wood. Sadly, the once-prized School One bell now lies forgotten and exposed to the weather at the Parker Press Building on Rahway Avenue. In 1999, the state-wide organization Preservation New Jersey placed School One on its list of most endangered sites in the state.

The Woodbridge school district has developed through the years into the largest district in Middlesex County with 16 elementary schools: Mawbey Street and Ross Street Schools in Woodbridge proper; Avenel Street and Woodbine Avenue in Avenel; Port Reading; Ford Avenue and Lafayette Estates in Fords;

"POOR FARM" C. 1910. The homeless and local persons serving sentences on municipal charges lived and worked at this homestead until 1920. It was located on the Free School Lands in Iselin. (Ruth Wolk)

Indian Avenue, Kennedy Park, and Robert Mascenik in Iselin; Menlo Park Terrace, Claremont Avenue, Oak Ridge Heights, Lynn Crest, and Pennsylvania Avenue in Colonia; and Matthew Jago School in Sewaren; 5 middle schools located in Avenel, Colonia, Fords, Iselin, and Woodbridge, and 3 high schools: Colonia, John F. Kennedy in Iselin, and Woodbridge, as well as an Adult High School in Colonia.

When Dr. Love retired as superintendent in 1933, Victor C. Nicklas succeeded him and continued in the position until his death in 1956, when Patrick A. Boylan took the helm. Dr. Reigh Carpenter, Dr. Fredric Buonocore, and Dr. Leroy Seitz have also headed the district in later years. Dr. Seitz left in 2000 to take another position and was followed briefly by Kenneth Kuchtyak, who resigned. In 2002, Vincent S. Smith is serving as acting superintendent until the board of education obtains a permanent replacement.

The controversial New Jersey State Report Cards issued in 2001 classified the Woodbridge schools as a middle-income socio-economic level district with a high majority of its elementary school and middle school students proficient in language, math, and science. On the high school level the scores for the year 2000 indicated that an average of 77 percent of the students were proficient in reading, mathematics, and writing. "Woodbridge Tech 2000," a public-private partnership, is working to bring state-of-the-art computer technology to all the schools in the township.

FIRST WHS CHEERLEADERS, 1927. From left to right (front row): Dorothy L. Leonard, Mina E. Danner, Director Robert E. Beach. (Back row): Captain Thomas J. Brennan, Edward C. Leeson. According to the 1927 Annual: "This squad has done quite a bit to liven up the games, and has tried to spell the athletics of Woodbridge High School with the three letter word, "Pep."

9. EXPANDING EXPRESSIONS OF FAITH: 1740 ONWARD

Now faith is the substance of things hoped for, the evidence of things not seen.
—Hebrews 11.1

The religious revival of the 1730s and 1740s known as the Great Awakening brought changes to the First Presbyterian Church in Woodbridge. After their earlier struggles to hire ministers, the members found an active pastor in Reverend John Pierson, who came to town in 1714. Pierson not only strengthened the local church and helped to increase its membership, but he also worked with the overall American Presbyterian Church to set up its leadership and seminaries separate from Europe and served as a founder of Princeton University.

Before Reverend Pierson left Woodbridge in 1752, he made plans for the members to apply for a charter to ensure that the local church lands (the Meeting House, parsonage properties, and the burial ground) would always be used as the original settlers intended. In 1756, the congregation applied for and received a Royal Charter from George II of England. The charter, which is still in the possession of the congregation, incorporated the church as the "First Presbyterian Church of Woodbridge."

The well-known Presbyterian clergyman and Woodbridge patriot Reverend Dr. Azel Roe began his 52-year pastorate in town in 1763. In addition, Reverend Roe rode on horseback to Metuchen to preach to the Presbyterians there, who were meeting in private homes. By 1767, the Metuchen congregation united with Woodbridge to share equally in the pastor's services until 1787.

The Episcopal church in town did not fare well during the early 1700s. Their small number of parishioners could not support the church they had built earlier, and by 1725, the building was in ruins. Members worshiped in private homes or traveled to St. Peter's Church in Perth Amboy for services. In 1756, Reverend Thomas Bradbury Chandler of Elizabethtown revitalized the parish and supervised the building of a new church at the same location as the earlier one.

Trinity Episcopal's second church was destroyed by a fire in a faulty woodstove in 1858. Through the tireless efforts of the parish's young rector Reverend Eugene Hoffman, a new building, the third and present church, was ready for consecration in May 1861. Eleven years later, the Church purchased Jonathan Dunham's colonial homestead for their rectory and remodeled the house, adding features in the then-popular Gothic Revival style. The Dunham house still serves as the rectory with one of Dunham's original millstones remaining on the property. Members of the Dunham family continue to live in the Woodbridge area today.

During the next 40 years, the church, one of the oldest parishes in New Jersey, established four branch churches in the township: St. John's in Fords and in Sewaren, St. Mark's in Carteret, and a church in Iselin, which later closed. Four guild units for parish women were organized in the 1920s as well as a Sunday school. The long-time rector, Father William Schmaus, came to the church in 1944 and directed the liquidation of the church mortgage in time for Trinity's 250th anniversary in May 1948.

President Harry S. Truman, King George VI of England, and other notables sent personal congratulations to the congregation. A joyous banquet concluded the anniversary festivities with many speakers including Mayor Greiner, Father Schmaus, two Episcopal bishops, vestry president James S. Wight, and master of ceremonies Merrill A. Mosher. Trinity Church flourishes at the present time and sponsors many outreach and community service programs, including a soup kitchen for the homeless.

Trinity Church possesses many valued artifacts, which are held for safekeeping in a local bank vault. These treasures include a 1751 folio Bible, one of ten copies of the first Prayer Book of the Episcopal Church in America (dated 1795), a 1760 sterling silver chalice, and an 1869 flagon and chalice.

Although church records indicate that as early as 1740 a small band of Methodists was meeting in Woodbridge homes, the Methodist Church did not become an important presence in town until the early 1800s. Founded at Oxford University in England in the 1730s by the Anglican clergyman John Wesley, Methodism spread slowly but steadily in America. Wesley's associate, Reverend George Whitefield, gave the first sermon to Woodbridge Methodists in 1740, while in 1792, Reverend Francis Asbury, the first American Methodist bishop and namesake of Asbury Park, New Jersey, preached in town.

On May 14, 1832, the Methodist Church notified its male members to meet at Strawberry Hill School to elect trustees and be incorporated as a "body politic." Before adjourning their first official meeting that day, the new trustees elected Nathan Harned as president, adopted the name "Methodist Episcopal Church" for their society, accepted a plan to build a meeting house on Main Street property offered by William Gage Inslee, appointed a building committee with instruction to "erect the frame immediately," and hired Isaac Prall as caretaker.

On July 3 of that year, the trustees gathered on the church grounds at 10 a.m. to raise the frame, hear an "appropriate discourse," and take up a collection of $9.33. By September, the 35-by-50–foot building was ready for dedication. A high white pulpit stood in the front of the sanctuary and a raised platform for the choir was located in the rear.

FIRST PRESBYTERIAN CHURCH C. 1920. For more than 325 years, a church has stood on this site on Rahway Avenue.

In 1842, James Valentine contributed property at 91 Main Street to build a parsonage, which was later sold to the Drake family. In 1870, the cornerstone was laid for a new church, and by 1888, a Sunday school building had been added. A new parsonage was built at 71 Main Street and still stands as a rental property for the Methodists.

On Wednesday evening, November 3, 1954, the Methodist church was almost demolished by fire. The front entrance and two beautiful stained-glass windows installed in 1870 were saved and incorporated into the restored church. Members held services at the Craftsmen's Club and at Congregation Adath Israel until the new building was consecrated in November 1956. No cause for the fire was ever found.

After the arrival of Reverend Theodore Seamans in 1958, the membership increased to over 500 members in the next ten years. Unfortunately, Reverend Seamans's active protest against the Vietnam War in the late 1960s and his invitation to a group of protesters from New York City to participate in a demonstration at the church caused a divisive controversy among the members. Many devoted Methodists left the church and ultimately, Reverend Seaman lost his pastorate. Reverend Galen Goodwin was appointed minister in 1970 and began the long task of rebuilding the congregation. Other ministers followed, and the Methodists today are again an active congregation.

During the nineteenth century, the First Presbyterian Church, often called the White Church, welcomed many new ministers, engaged in an active building program, and endured some tribulations. In 1803, the congregation replaced their century-old Meeting House with a new church designed and built by Jonathan Freeman. Reverend Roe died in 1815 after 52 years of service in town. In 1818, three church ladies organized the first Sunday school in the state.

Serious difficulties arose between the congregation and the session (trustees) of the church in 1873. When Reverend Joseph M. McNulty took the pulpit the following year, 38 members, including several elders, resigned. Although the Presbyterians and Congregationalists share a common heritage from English Puritanism, they differed on the governing of the local church. The local Presbyterians weathered the storm and by 1877 were moving forward with new programs. The church continues as a thriving presence in town, and its soaring, white spire remains an enduring landmark.

The former Presbyterians officially organized the Congregational Church in September 1874 at the home of John White with Brewster, Campbell, Cutter, Dally, Demarest, Edgar, Freeman, Kelly, Lockwood, Melick, Osborn, and Voorhees family members among the founders. The new church incorporated in January 1875 and met at the old Masonic Hall until the members built their own church on the corner of Barron and Grove Avenues.

Several ministers shepherded the congregation until the well-known Reverend William V.D. Strong arrived in the 1920s and served the church for a quarter century. Some years ago the congregation affiliated with the United Church of Christ.

By mid-nineteenth century, the growing Catholic population knew it was time to build a church in town, and in 1865 their wooden framed chapel on the south side of Main Street near Metuchen Avenue became a reality. Father Quinn, who had spearheaded the project, celebrated the first Mass. In 1871, the chapel became a mission of the Church of Saint Mary's in Perth Amboy with their pastor, Reverend Peter L. Connolly, administering to the Woodbridge church as well. The first resident pastor, Reverend Stephen Bettoni from Hoboken, arrived in 1878 and confirmed 35 boys and 31 girls the following year, a joyous testament to the strength and vitality of the new church.

When Reverend James A. Walsh took over the parish a few years later, he soon realized that his parishioners were quickly outgrowing their small chapel. Reverend Walsh purchased property across Main Street from the chapel for a new church and rectory but was transferred before he could carry out his plans. A previous parish priest, Father James F. Devine, returned to officiate at the laying of the cornerstone in 1887 and at the consecration of the new house of worship the following year. The church was named for one of the apostles of Jesus, St. James the Younger or the Less, who was so named to distinguish him from St. James the Greater, the brother of St. John.

Now Father Devine looked toward building a school and convent and invited the Sisters of Mercy to take charge. Mother Mary Joseph and Sisters Mary Veronica, Mary Baptist, and Mary Anacletus arrived in September 1890 from their motherhouse in Bordentown, New Jersey, enthusiastic to begin their teaching ministry in Woodbridge. The original chapel was transformed into St. James School, which opened that fall with 100 students.

The Knights of Columbus, a fraternal order of Roman Catholic men founded in 1882 in New Haven, Connecticut, was chartered in town in 1904 as the Middlesex Council and in 1921 purchased their present clubhouse on Main Street at Amboy Avenue, formerly the Elias family's private home. A shrine to Our Lady of Fatima, formerly an old well, still stands on the clubhouse property as a devotional landmark.

The year 1922 marked the beginning of Court Mercedes at St. James, the 769th Court of Catholic Daughters in America, an active group to this day. Ninety charter members gathered to pursue spiritual, patriotic, intellectual, and charitable goals under the direction of their first grand regent, Mrs. Edward Flanagan. During World War II, the ladies served Sunday breakfast to the servicemen and women at Camp Kilmer in Edison Township.

In 1924, St. James' Church was moved from Main Street to the corner of Amboy Avenue and Grove Street. This labor-intensive project took many weeks to complete. Tractors pulled the building forward, a few feet at a time. It was reported that this massive undertaking marked the first time in the United States that such a large building was moved by tractors, instead of horses. The present St. James' School was completed in 1924.

METHODIST EPISCOPAL CHURCH C. 1920. A fire in 1954 nearly destroyed this building on Main Street, whose congregation is known today as the United Methodist Church.

The well-known Reverend Charles G. McCorristin came to town in 1937 and continued officiating at St. James until his death in 1966. His Holiness Pope Pius XII appointed him a domestic prelate in 1948 with the title Right Reverend Monsignor. In 1965, Father McCorristin and Bishop George W. Ahr of the Diocese of Trenton initiated plans for a completely new St. James' Church. Sadly, construction was delayed because of the illness and death of Father McCorristin. Monsignor Maurice P. Griffin assumed supervision for the building of the imposing church, which stands on the corner of Amboy Avenue and Main Street, the historic crossroads of Woodbridge. The new house of worship, seating 1,200, was designed to incorporate traditional features of Romanesque architecture into a simple, contemporary style with deeply recessed stained-glass windows. The tall, lighted bell tower houses the original bell from old St. James as well as added clarion tones. Today, the St. James' parish sponsors a gala fair in the fall on Main Street with displays and booths from many local organizations and township offices. Under the direction of principal Rosemarie Del Corio, St. James' School continues as a flourishing pre-K-8 school of 350 students with the majority of the graduates attending area Catholic secondary schools.

The turn of the century saw new houses of worship opening in town, reflecting the growing diversity of Woodbridge's population. Reverend Gabriel Dokus of Connecticut founded the Hungarian Reformed Church in 1904 with Reverend Alexander Vajo from Hungary as the first minister. In March 1904, the

ST. JAMES'S CHURCH. Built in the 1960s, this large, contemporary edifice stands at the corner of Main Street and Amboy Avenue.

congregation purchased five lots and initiated a fund-raising project, which materialized into a church building two years later on School Street, next to School One. By 1922, the congregation had added a Sunday school and recreation building and organized a Ladies' Aid Society.

In December 1938, Reverend Laszlo Egry from Ohio was called to the pastorate and under him a parsonage was built and the church remodeled. Reverend Laszlo Kecskemethy came to serve the parish in 1945 and introduced worship services and Sunday school classes in English. Reverend Egry later returned to town and presided over the dedication of a new church in 1962. The Hungarian Reformed Church continues as an active ministry today.

The First Baptist Church of Woodbridge, an African-American congregation organized in 1906, purchased property from the Cutter family on Nielson Street for their first building. In 1957, members constructed a larger church on their original site, and in the 1990s moved to an unused school building in Sewaren, which they are presently refurbishing to accommodate their expanding membership.

Hungarian immigrants also founded the Roman Catholic Church of Our Lady of Mount Carmel on Amboy Avenue in 1920. The parishioners volunteered many hours of service to help build a church, parish hall, and rectory by 1938. Two years later the congregation welcomed Crown Prince Otto, son of dethroned King Charles of Hungary. The prince attended devotions and a reception, where he was greeted by Mayor Greiner. When a new building was completed, the old sanctuary was converted into a parochial school, which saw the graduation of its first eighth-grade class of 12 students in 1966. The school continued until 1970, when the teaching sisters were unexpectedly withdrawn.

After 30 years of dedicated service, Father Vincent S. Lenyi retired because of failing health. An ardent Hungarian patriot, Reverend Lenyi welcomed Hungarian immigrants arriving in the United States after World War II. He provided them with temporary housing in the parish hall as well as with food and clothing, and located jobs for them. Two well-known Hungarian religious leaders visited the parish, Cardinal József Mindszenty in 1974, and Cardinal Ladislaus Paskai in 1989. Cardinal Mindszenty symbolized the Hungarians' struggle for freedom from communism. Today the church sponsors many organizations, including the Rosary Society, Mount Carmel Catholic War Veterans, and an active Confraternity of Christian Doctrine (CCD) program for children.

In the fall of 1907, a small group of local Jewish families met at Kendal's Hall, near where the cloverleaf intersection was later built, to pray for the high holidays of Rosh Hashanah and Yom Kippur. This meeting marked the beginning of Congregation Adath Israel. Israel Belaty, Bernath Krauss, Joseph Lefkowitz, Abraham Duff, and Sam Haas signed the congregation's certificate of incorporation, which was filed in December 1913. In 1914, Levy Najavits, a storekeeper, milk distributor, and a Hebrew scholar, was named lay leader of the congregation with part-time rabbis engaged for the High Holy Days. Mr. Najavits's wife became the first president of the sisterhood in 1923.

The corporation moved forward to erect a building in town to hold religious services and instruction in accordance with the Hebrew faith. Joseph Ostrowicz donated a lot next to School One on School Street for the synagogue, which was completed in 1923. Prior to that time, the congregation met at Feuchtman's farm on Metuchen Avenue, in the loft of Choper's Department Store and at the *Independent-Leader* building.

The year 1948 marked the consecration of the cornerstone for the new Adath Israel Synagogue and Community Center on Amboy Avenue near Woodbridge Park on land donated by local businessman Abraham J. Neiss. Speakers at the celebration included State Assemblyman Bernard W. Vogel, David T. Wilentz, Mayor Greiner, Charles E. Gregory, Reverend William A. Schmaus, and Dr. Henry A. Belafsky, who was president of the congregation at that time.

Congregation Adath Israel celebrated its 50th anniversary with a joyous reception and dinner-dance on March 14, 1964, with Mrs. Sol Klein and Jack Laden as co-chairpersons. An illustrated program with historical highlights was published for the occasion. At that time, there were 229 members and a Hebrew school with 106 students in five grades. The congregation marked its 65th anniversary on March 27, 1978, and continues today as an active and involved segment of the Woodbridge community.

As Woodbridge moves into the twenty-first century, the local houses of worship are alive and well and add greatly to the collective spirit and cohesiveness that help Woodbridge continue as a thriving municipality.

JOYOUS OCCASION, JUNE 20, 1948. Woodbridge Park was the scene of the dedication of the cornerstone of the new Congregation Adath Israel Synagogue and Community Center on Amboy Avenue. State senator Bernard J. Vogel (Standing on platform) was among the speakers.

10. COMMUNITIES WITHIN

The world is on the move, and never before at such a pace! —Mary Hart Pattison, (from *Colonia Yesterday*)

AVENEL

Until the late 1800s, Avenel, like many sections of the township, grew slowly. For years, the Avenel landscape comprised an area of open meadows, two fishing ponds, and groves of weeping willows. The village's early name, Demarest on the Hill, can be traced to Captain Demarest, a descendent of a colonial family. Demarest is credited with founding the community and naming it for his daughter, Avenel. An 1867 township map indicates "Proposed Avanel Station," which uses a slightly different spelling, but certainly refers to the captain's daughter. The town was officially established in 1901. The first settlers included members of the Brown, Clark, Cooper, Crowell, Douglass, Edgar, and Thorpe families, along with the Demarests.

Protestants living in the village organized a union Sunday school in 1871, which met at several locations until they started a Presbyterian church in 1927. John M. Clark, pioneering resident and relative of Abraham Clark (a New Jersey signer of the Declaration of Independence), served as Sunday school superintendent until 1895. Three years later, the members built the Demarest Union Chapel and in 1930 dedicated the First Presbyterian Church of Avenel. In 1987, the congregation celebrated its 60th anniversary with a homecoming observance and a special visit from Reverend Dr. Charles S. MacKenzie, who served as the minister of the church from 1954 to 1964. The members adopted a "sister church," the Iglesia Evangelica Dominicana, in the Dominican Republic in 1988.

The massive, domed stronghold, which was known for years as the Rahway Reformatory or the Rahway State Prison, is actually located in Avenel on Rahway Avenue. Originally named the New Jersey Reformatory, today's East Jersey State Prison is a maximum-security facility with a prison population of about 2,400 men. The state legislature began plans in 1895 to build a reformatory on Woodbridge land known as the Edgar Farm. The first inmates, young men guilty of a first crime, arrived on August 5, 1901.

Avenel Fire Department, 1922. Built about 1919, this firehouse stood on the corner of Hyatt and Ziegler Streets. Chief Florian Wranitz stands on the truck at right. (Edward Berardi)

The first PRR station in Avenel was designed in Victorian style on the west side of the tracks and included an apartment on the second floor and beautifully groomed grounds. An underpass replaced the grade crossing on Avenel Street in 1940 and a new station was built. In 1992, New Jersey Transit made plans to close the Avenel station, but through the efforts of township Councilman Frank Pelzman and Mayor Jim McGreevey, the Avenel station remains open. New Jersey Transit spent $1.9 million on improvements with additional parking and accessibility for people with disabilities.

Beginning in 1906, the first Jewish families, the Sterns, Demblings, Foxes, Grossmans, and Schillers, held religious services in their homes and later at the Avenel Hotel on Remsen Avenue. Finally, the congregation built a synagogue, B'nai Jacob, on Lord Street, which was open in its first years only on the High Holy Days. The temple has steadily expanded with Hebrew school classes, an active sisterhood, choir, men's club, and youth groups.

Joseph Szabo served as first fire chief when Avenel Fire Company No. 1 was formed in 1913. The charter members purchased a 70-gallon chemical hand-drawn apparatus. With the help of public-minded citizens, the company built a hollow brick firehouse in 1919, and a much larger one in 1929 at the corner of Avenel Street and Route One. New firetrucks and alarm systems have been added through the years.

The Woman's Club began in 1920 and founded the first free public library, which originated as a circulating library in a private home. The library expanded into the Community House, then the railroad station waiting room, where glass bookcases lined the walls, and finally into its own building.

St. Andrew's Roman Catholic Church was organized in 1921 as a mission of St. James Church. Parishioners celebrated Mass at the Avenel School until 1939, when their first building was consecrated by Monsignor Charles G. McCorristin. Reverend Charles Dusten served as St. Andrew's first pastor from 1941 until his untimely death three years later. Reverend John J. Eagan took his place and supervised the building of a new church in 1956.

With more than 15,000 people, Avenel is one of the township's larger subdivisions. Although it has developed into a busy residential area with very little open space left, Avenel still is a friendly place to live, shop, and enjoy church and community activities.

COLONIA

According to David T. Miller's history of Colonia, seven hamlets located entirely or partially in today's Colonia comprised the original settlement: the farming village of Houghtonville (also spelled Houghtenville); Six Roads, situated at the intersection of St. George's Avenue (earlier known as the King's Highway and King George's Post Road), Colonia Boulevard, and State Route 27, where previously six roads met; Milton, which became part of Rahway after 1860; New Dover, a colonial village located where New Dover Road crosses Wood Avenue; Leesville, founded by the enterprising Lee family of merchants and manufacturers, and now part of southeastern Rahway; Pleasant Mills, of which little is known, except that its location is believed to have been behind the Henry Inman Library; and Locust Grove or Locust Hill, on Lake Avenue at the Clark border.

The Lake, Inman, and Wood families were among the earliest settlers and several roads carry their names today. The portrait painter and landscapist Henry Inman (1801–1846), who was born in New York State, later lived with relatives in the Inman Avenue section of today's Colonia. Henry Inman was among the first artists to study the techniques of lithography, a process similar to printing. Inman's endearing portrait *The Children of Bishop Doane* (1835) is one of five of the artist's paintings in the permanent collection of the Newark Museum.

After traveling to Rahway, Metuchen, and Woodbridge for services, members of the Toms, Wood, Badgley, Payne, Noe, and Force families organized the New Dover Methodist Church in 1847. The church, which is now located about 1,000 feet over the Colonia border on New Dover Road in Edison, has steadily expanded.

Most of present-day Colonia remained a rural outreach until the late nineteenth century when well-to-do New Yorkers carved out a community of gracious, spacious homes, many named to express their owners' personal and poetic sentiments. Edward S. Savage purchased " 'Neath Oaks," built earlier by George P. Gordon, owner of Gordon Printing Press in Rahway. A towering oak tree near a blacksmith shop on the property had prompted the original name, which Savage changed to "Bel Air." Entrepreneur Edward G. Cone and his family moved from a New York City brownstone to "The Trees," a 60-acre colonial farm in Houghtonville. Cone built several homes on his land and named the development "The Colony." The Cones are also credited with introducing the name Colonia to replace Houghtonville. When discussing the change in later years, daughter Elizabeth Cone is quoted as saying, "It is a precious place with a pitiful name. The very sound suggests hungry dogs! . . . It just had to be changed . . ."[1]

George Neville, president of the Cotton Exchange, called his home "Sewania" while William and Eva Rollinson initiated a local contest to name their new, imposing mansion. The winning name, "Devonshire," reflected pastoral scenes in Devon, England.

The first house built on the land developed by the Cones was purchased by Mary and Frank Pattison, who named it "The House o' Four Winds." When the Cones' son Edward Kinnekort Cone and his bride, Helen Savage (of the "Bel Air" estate), moved into their new home in 1904, they called it "Kinnekort," a Dutch surname from the family of Mr. Cone's mother.

To enhance the elegance of their new community, Edward G. Cone and fellow investors purchased an extra 50 acres to construct the Colonia Country Club with a nine-hole golf course. The club opened in 1899. The Adams homestead on the property became the clubhouse, which continued in use until 1966, when the present building replaced it. In 1923, Cone added 55 acres to expand the course to 18 holes.

When Colonia resident and outstanding orthopedic surgeon Edward Houdlett Albee, M.D. was named the first civilian director of a proposed U.S. Army hospital during World War I, he began a nationwide search for a suitable location. Quite by chance, he and Charles D. Freeman, who also lived in Colonia and held vast acreage there, met on a train to New York. Dr. Albee told Freeman about his quest for a hospital site, and immediately Freeman offered to lease 200 acres of his property to the U.S. government for the hospital. Dr. Albee accepted his offer and shortly thereafter persuaded the government to open General Hospital No. 3 in Colonia for all veterans returning from "the war to end all wars," who required orthopedic treatment for their injuries.

The hospital opened in 1918 and contained 110 barracks-type buildings with 18 single-story wards, 5 mess halls and kitchens, a central heating plant, telephone exchanges, a swimming pool, libraries, and a newspaper entitled *Over Here*. Chief Surgeon Albee performed many of the bone graft operations himself, using techniques that were uniquely his own. Out of 6,000 servicemen treated, only 17 died at the hospital. On October 15, 1919, the Army closed the complex and razed most of the buildings.

Dr. Albee (1876–1945), a native of Maine, and his wife, Louella Berry Albee, a relative of clay merchant William H. Berry, maintained "Blythmoor," an estate in Colonia. The mansion's many amenities included a built-in pipe organ and the largest dining room in town. "Blythmoor" was torn down in the 1980s and replaced by several private homes. After receiving his medical degree in 1903 from

Harvard University, where he specialized in orthopedics, Dr. Albee performed the first bone graft operation. Through the years, his reputation grew as a result of his pioneering orthopedic procedures. He headed the New Jersey Rehabilitation Commission for 20 years and was awarded the New Jersey Distinguished Service Cross in 1939. Dr. Albee wrote his autobiography, *A Surgeon's Fight to Rebuild Men*, which included a foreword by Lowell Thomas, the well-known radio commentator and author:

> They call him the "Burbank of Surgery," and even his colleagues and contemporaries look upon him literally as a miracle man. It is a definite fact that thousands of men today are walking about and enjoying their strength only because Fred Albee discovered how to graft human bone, thousands who would otherwise be either crippled or dead. If we search through the entire history of the science that he has practiced so magnificently, we shall find few single contributions of greater importance or even as great. But that is not all. He has evolved at least a hundred new operations in the healing of men and women.

Mary Hart Pattison (1869–1951) surely holds her place as another of Colonia's illustrious citizens and a champion of women's rights. Born in Brooklyn, New York, she grew up in Metuchen and was educated at public and private schools. Mrs. Pattison, who was often called Molly, married Frank Ambler Pattison in 1893 and settled in Colonia in 1908. Her husband, a Rutgers University graduate, owned a mechanical and electrical engineering consulting firm in New York.

Mary and Frank Pattison supported the far-reaching ideals of the Progressive Party, an early-twentieth-century movement that advanced improvement for the poor, prison reform, women's rights, conservation of natural resources, and world peace. Mrs. Pattison was elected president of the New Jersey Federation of

U.S. ARMY HOSPITAL IN COLONIA, 1918. *Directed by Dr. Fred H. Albee, this remarkable hospital treated returning World War I veterans. (Robert Rippen)*

Women's Clubs (NJFWC) in 1909 and in 1912 served on the State Committee of the Progressive Party:

> Pattison's chief motivation for her political work was her belief that women's true calling was homemaking, but that the role of homemaker had to be made more socially responsible, efficient, interesting, and creative in order to appeal to the many college educated women being attracted away from the home by new career choices. To this end, she concentrated her efforts in the field of "domestic engineering."[2]

In June 1910, she opened a State Housekeeping Experiment Station in a separate service house, the "Maisonette," located next door to her Colonia home. The station was sponsored by the NJFWC. Mrs. Pattison's goals were to lessen the high cost of living, alleviate the shortage of domestic workers, and remove the endless toil of housework. The Colonia Civic Circle, whose members included Jenny Cochran, Helen Savage Cone, Elizabeth, Kate, and Grace Cone, Sarah Krug, Louella Albee, and Mamie Neville, worked at the station during its year of operation. The women tried out many sources of energy, baking ovens, and other cooking utensils, as well as an electric motor to power household appliances. Through her experiments, Mary Pattison fostered time-motion studies for household tasks and espoused the importance of beautiful surroundings within the home. She described her experiences in *The Principles of Domestic Engineering*, published in 1914. She envisioned her ideas as a way of transforming and diminishing housework so that everyone, men and women alike, would have time and energy to devote to broader humanitarian concerns. "Pattison and the Federation of Women's Clubs were very much ahead of their time."[3]

When she was 80 years old, Mrs. Pattison wrote *Colonia Yesterday*, a history of her beloved community. The author's humor and clear eye for the nuances that made Colonia such a unique, beautiful, and privileged place provide readers today with a lively chronicle of another time. The Junto, a civic-minded club of local women, was organized about 1938 and sponsored the publication of *Colonia Yesterday* in 1951. The Cone, Albee, Freeman, and Pattison families, and those associated with them, left a lasting legacy for Colonia. Their vision was guided by the preservation of the natural environment, devoted service to the community, and an enjoyment of gracious living.

The early twentieth century saw the beginnings of the Catholic church in the Colonia area. The first mass was said in 1913 on Charles Freeman's estate. Freeman honored his Irish employees' request for religious services by contacting the headquarters of the Trenton Diocese for a clergyman and opening a caretaker's cottage on his property to house the services. A priest traveled by train each Sunday from Trenton and was met at the Colonia PRR Station by a horse and carriage or a sleigh to carry him to the Freeman estate.

A few years later, the Catholic Church designated the Colonia-Iselin area as a mission of St. Mary's Church in South Amboy. In October 1919, Monsignor

FORDS WOMEN'S CLUB ON STAGE, 1927. One of the many joyous memories shared by the members was their presentation of a play entitled Women, the Silent Sufferer. *(Mary Molnar)*

Griffin of South Amboy purchased the Nurses' Recreation Hall from U.S. General Hospital No. 3 and arranged for it to be moved in sections to the corner of Middlesex Avenue and Oak Tree Road in Iselin. After it was reassembled, the hall served as St. Cecelia's Church until it was torn down in 1953. By 1959, the many parishioners who came from Colonia, Iselin, and Edison had outgrown their Iselin buildings. Bishop George Ahr divided the parish and assigned Reverend Walter Radziwon as Colonia's first priest. He held masses at the Hoffman Boulevard School. Colonia's new congregation, named St. John Vianney, grew rapidly with several buildings on Inman Avenue dedicated in 1961.

The years leading up to World War I ushered in the first of Colonia's many civic, fraternal, and charitable organizations. Local ladies organized the Mercy Committee, an affiliate of the American Red Cross, to provide relief to war-torn European countries. In 1917, they helped sufferers closer to home who had been injured or left homeless after the Morgan, New Jersey Munitions explosion, and later with the rehabilitation of World War I veterans. The members of Colonia Citizens, Inc. first met in 1932 to aid residents during the Depression. The group started a market to sell homemade goods and published Colonia's first newspaper, the *Colonia Sun*. American Legion Post Number 248 met for the first time in 1935, while the Colonia Civic Improvement Club, organized in 1936, established the first firehouse in 1943, and spearheaded the paving of streets in the Inman Avenue section. Margaret Soulé, wife of Dr. Robert Soulé, an orthopedic surgeon at St. Elizabeth's Hospital, and her library committee were the moving force behind the founding of the Colonia Public Library in 1939. Before it opened, Mrs. Soulé acted as a traveling library, hand delivering books to residents that she thought they would enjoy reading. And apparently they did!

Jewish residents formed Temple Beth Am, and dedicated their first building in 1963. In the 1970s the temple was renamed Ohev Shalom and flourishes today with a growing congregation of more than 90 families.

David T. Miller has written that after the development initiated by the Cone family, Colonia's rapid residential growth slowed from time to time, depending on national and world events. Today Colonia's more than 18,000 people make it the largest of the towns within Woodbridge Township.

Many civic and taxpayers' associations arose among the new homeowners to confront issues of safety, schools, and property values. Colonia Associates, Inc. organized in 1945 for one purpose: to change the proposed route of the Garden State Parkway so that the road would not cut Colonia in half. At numerous meetings in Trenton, the members presented alternate plans for realignment and finally convinced the State to change the path of the parkway to its present location.

The best-kept secret in Colonia, and probably in all of Woodbridge, was the existence of a casino from 1943 to 1951 in an old house known as "Linden Farms" and later as the "Lone Star Ranch." The casino property was razed in 1960 and replaced by the Darlow Village residential development. The casino straddled the counties of Middlesex and Union enabling the high-rollers to quickly cross the county line and be out of harm's way should the authorities be spotted on the grounds. (See Miller's history of Colonia for an entertaining, "virtual" visit to this hidden, local hotspot.)

FORDS

This large section of town, with more than 14,000 people today, may have been named for one of its first colonists, John Ford, who arrived in 1686. However, it may have come by its name in the late 1800s when a merchant named Ford opened a general store on New Brunswick Avenue at Main Street. Neighbors called the location Ford's Corner, which was later shortened to Fords.

Several nationalities settled in Fords during the nineteenth century. Clay mining drew many immigrants from Germany, Poland, Hungary, and Czechoslovakia. Others arrived from the Scandinavian countries to establish dairy farms and carpentry and woodworking businesses. The Grosses are thought to be the first Jewish family in Fords. They settled in the Sand Hills area in 1890 and opened a grocery store.

The St. Nicholas Byzantine Catholic Church was one of the earliest churches organized in Fords. Under the name of St. Octa Nikolaja Greek Catholic

Congregation, the church received a charter in 1898 and purchased land on Second Street, where the church stands today. Members of the Dudics, Ondrik, Choma, Hegyes, Yakubik, Demscak, Smoliga, Gulya, Suha, and Chinchar families were among the founders.

Danish residents organized a Sunday school in 1908 and built a chapel in 1909, events which marked the beginning of Our Redeemer Lutheran Church. They also conducted occasional services in Danish under Reverend L. Kreyling, who came in 1919 to serve as pastor. Today the church, which is located at Fourth Street and Ford Avenue, is part of the Missouri Synod of the Lutheran Church and conducts a Christian Day School with classes from kindergarten through sixth grade. After new buildings were added to the church, the original chapel was moved to Corrielle Street to serve as the Fords Public Library and as the clubhouse for the Women's Club of Fords.

In 1919 Roman Catholics in Fords established the mission of Our Lady of Peace through St. Mary's church in Perth Amboy and celebrated their first mass at the Fairfield School. The parishioners purchased land on Amboy Avenue and celebrated mass and conducted church activities in a temporary Quonset hut erected on the property. A combination church and school was built in 1928 on nearby land with the parish school opening in 1930. Several priests officiated at Our Lady of Peace until Father John Grimes was named pastor in 1947. The parish expanded considerably under Father Grimes and continued to grow under his successor, Monsignor Joseph R. Brzozowski, known familiarly as "Monsignor

OLD FORDS C. 1910. This early postcard pictured a local residence on the left and the Fords post office and grocery store on the right.

111

Joe." The Very Reverend Robert J. Zamorski followed the monsignor in 1986. During his pastorate many improvements were made to the church and the school. Our Lady of Peace grew in 75 years from 75 families to more than 3,000 families.

Members of the First Presbyterian Church, earlier known as the Slovak Presbyterian Church, laid the cornerstone for their building on Hoy Avenue in 1926. Local immigrants worked tirelessly to bring their congregation to life, and in the early years shared a minister with the Slovak Presbyterian Church of Perth Amboy. In 1961, the church became the First Presbyterian Church of Fords with services in English only.

Other active Fords churches today include St. John's Episcopal Church on Hoy Avenue, for whom the St. John's First Aid Squad of Fords is named, and Grace Baptist Church on King George Road.

In 1916, a movement was initiated to annex Fords, Keasbey, and Hopelawn to the City of Perth Amboy, but the state assembly bill was never approved. The matter was eventually dropped.

Returning servicemen of Fords broke ground for a Veterans of Foreign Wars post home. In 1950, the members dedicated a monument in memory of all World War II soldiers who lost their lives in the conflict.

At the time of the New Jersey Tercentenary in 1964, 37 children from Fords School #7 compiled a history of the community entitled *Fords, Yesterday and Today*

HOPELAWN LANDMARK. This whimsical terra cotta mosaic, created by a local clay company, depicts the Old Woman in the Shoe (who had so many children she didn't know what to do), and once decorated a local shoe repair shop on Florida Grove Road. It remains in its original location, which is now a private home. (Ray J. Schneider)

under the direction of Dorothy F.D. Ludewig, principal of the school. The students researched all aspects of Fords history, including transportation, immigration, churches, schools, services, businesses, sports, and organizations. Complete with vintage photographs, the booklet stands today as a comprehensive document of the town from its beginning through 1964.

Fords has evolved as a miniature melting pot of many nationalities living and working together. Today most of the town is comprised of residences with a thriving business district on New Brunswick Avenue.

HOPELAWN

Hopelawn was a farming area settled by the Luther Hope family. By the late 1800s, Hope's Lawn was shortened to Hopelawn. At 0.4 square miles, it is the smallest of the township's subdivisions. The village made the headlines on August 24, 1941, when a funnel-shaped twister tore through Hopelawn, demolishing or severely damaging 57 houses in a quarter-mile-wide and 4-mile-long path of destruction. Police, firemen, and nearby first aid squads rescued the injured. No one was killed.

Several local organizations established a library in Hopelawn during the 1940s on Howard Street in a building donated by Mr. and Mrs. John Hladik. Citizens donated their time and money to open the library, which started with a collection of 2,000 books. Later efforts to move to a new library never materialized, and today residents use the other branches of the Woodbridge Library System.

Hopelawn has remained a residential community through the years with ties to nearby Perth Amboy. Many of its early residents were European immigrants involved in the clay industry and attended various ethnic churches in Perth Amboy where their native languages were spoken.

The Hopelawn School, Number Ten, also known as the Ellendale Terrace School, opened in 1914 and closed many years later. Students today are bussed to other township schools. The Hopelawn Veterans of Foreign Wars (VFW), one of several VFW chapters in the township, maintains a clubhouse and an active chapter in town. Its members volunteer at the new Veterans' Home in Menlo Park, planning many social functions for the residents.

ISELIN

Iselin was originally known as Perrytown, possibly named for John W. Perry, a farmer and Revolutionary War soldier. During the Civil War, Perrytown was called Uniontown, a name that arose when sections of Iselin and Colonia became a thoroughfare for moving Union soldiers to points north and south. With plentiful fresh water, grassy fields, and leafy trees, the area was designated an official camp for the troops and quite naturally acquired the name Uniontown.

After the war, Adrian George Iselin, New York businessman and personal friend of President Theodore Roosevelt, purchased land on the east end of Green

Street in Uniontown. The retired governess of his seven children, Mrs. L. Matthews, wanted to open a private school for wealthy young ladies from New York City, and Mr. Iselin stepped in to finance the project. To honor her benefactor, Mrs. Matthews named the school Adrian's Young Ladies' Seminary. The finishing school operated successfully for a number of years with a curriculum centering on the preparation of young women to join New York society. In 1877, a fire demolished the school, which never reopened. Remains of the campus and a nearby open well were visible until the construction of John F. Kennedy Memorial High School in 1964.

Iselin also built an ornate railroad station along the tracks of the PRR to enable the students to step off the city train into a beautiful, wooded environment en route to the seminary. Later the name Iselin appeared in bold letters on the station, and as time went by, Uniontown evolved into Iselin. Mr. Iselin himself never lived in the village.

The first stores arrived in Iselin in 1918, when the Mastrangelo family opened a small general store in their home on Chain o'Hills Road. Other establishments included Frank Moscarelli's Grocery on Middlesex Avenue, Ciccone's Barbershop on Oak Tree Road, Leo Murphy's Butcher Shop, Petoletti's Pharmacy, and Oliver's Tavern.

Mr. Iselin's business district fell on bad times during the 1970s, the heyday of the mammoth malls and large highway stores moving into the area. As the local shops went out of business, the downtown area became unsafe and a hangout for motorcycle gangs. A *New York Times* article of April 21, 2002 describes Iselin's metamorphosis since that time:

> But a closer look reveals that Iselin, one of nine areas that make up Woodbridge Township, is not your run-of-the-mill bedroom community. In the last decade, the downtown business district of the Middlesex County hamlet—centered at Oak Tree Road and Green Street—has become a thriving, retail mecca for Indians, who flock here to dine on authentic Indian food and to shop in the many Indian groceries, jewelry stores and sari shops.[4]

Shopkeepers from India were first attracted to Iselin by the low rents for storefronts, but in the beginning, they were almost driven out by vandalism. They persisted, however, and as more stores opened, the streets became safer. An additional lot and the widening of the main street have partially alleviated a serious parking problem, but heavy traffic through Iselin continues to cause congestion and delays.

Iselin's transformation has brought about a booming real estate market with approximately 16,000 people living in the community. Many people who grew up in town have stayed on to raise their own children there. Residents are active in the community, and Iselin Middle School and JFK High School are both involved in the National Service Learning Leader school program where students

ISELIN STATION C. 1935. Adrian George Iselin built the imposing PRR station in the late 1800s for the young ladies arriving from New York City to attend his Iselin finishing school.

volunteer in such projects as building a playground at Merrill Park, helping the homeless, and supporting a children's hospital.

KEASBEY

The community of Keasbey was founded in 1882, when brothers Edward, Anthony Q., and George M. Keasbey founded the Raritan Hollow and Porous Brick Company and probably gave the village its name. The Carborundum Company's huge plant opened in 1891 and its distinctive sign is still visible to southbound motorists crossing the Garden State Parkway bridge. Because of its important location on the Raritan River, the town prospered as a clay-mining center for many years.

European immigrants, especially from Hungary and Poland, settled in town to fill the clay-related jobs. They built Polish- and Hungarian-speaking churches and shared in the camaraderie of the now-defunct Keasbey Eagles Club, a social and athletic association.

Keasbey was also home to the Florida Grove Beach, which operated as a resort and picnic grove until early in the twentieth century, when it was taken over by the clay industry. Public school Number Eight, built by Joseph McEwen (grandfather of author Robert J. McEwen), opened in 1908 and closed in later years because of declining enrollment. Today students are bussed to classes in Fords and to Woodbridge High School.

KEASBEY LANDMARK C. 1960. For many years the Carborundum Company, a manufacturer of abrasive tools, dominated the Keasbey waterfront of the Raritan River.

After World War II, however, much of Keasbey's land was appropriated for highways, including the intersection of Interstate Highway 287 and an expansion of State Route 440. The township's municipal garage, storage tanks for the Hess Corporation, and a cement manufacturing plant are also part of Keasbey's landscape today.

A diversified population that includes African Americans and Spanish-speaking immigrants now defines Keasbey. As these residents become more established, the town will undoubtedly branch out in new directions.

MENLO PARK TERRACE

Bordering on the Garden State Parkway and Route One near Iselin, the community known as Menlo Park Terrace developed a separate identity after World War II when many new homes and an elementary school were built there. During the Revolutionary War, a copper mine known as Mine Gully operated nearby, and in 1876 Thomas Alva Edison, the area's most famous resident, arrived. He established his laboratory and experimental electrical station in that part of present-day Edison known as Menlo Park.

PORT READING

Port Reading was first settled around 1700 by homesteading families whose names included Blair, Brown, Haddon, Bunn, Crowell, Pierce, Fitz Randolph, Tappen, and Vernon. Farming was their quiet way of life until the late 1800s when major changes suddenly transformed this rural retreat into a noisy, bustling coal-shipping terminal. In 1890, the president of the Reading Railroad, Archibald A. McLeod, began searching for better terminal facilities from which his railroad could ship its coal and freight. He concluded that the best way to accomplish this goal would be to build a terminal near New York City.

McLeod and his chief engineer decided that the Woodbridge land fronting on the deep waters of Arthur Kill would be ideal and authorized the company to buy the necessary parcels of land for the terminal. By 1892, Charles A. Link of the railroad's real estate department had quietly purchased over 300 acres of farm and waterfront property before anyone suspected what had happened. The Port Reading Railroad was quickly incorporated, and a right of way from Bound Brook was put in place to the new terminal. Suddenly this previously unnamed outpost that people traveled through to get to Blazing Star Landing had its own place name. As the port at the terminus of the Reading Railroad, it was now the bona-fide village of Port Reading.

Lawrence J. Barrett, the railroad's plant manager and shipping agent, quickly turned Port Reading into a company town. Immigrants from Italy moved in to fill the new jobs and needed living quarters and community services. The company constructed barracks near the docks for the laborers and located temporary housing in other parts of Woodbridge for office and railroad employees. Barrett persuaded Woodbridge authorities to pave the local roads, introduce city water and electricity, organize a police force, and build a large school.

The Port Reading Terminal grew rapidly. By 1897, the company built a second pier and storage for 1,000 additional railroad cars and a few years later authorized the double tracking of the original pier, another large coal pier, and more storage. In 1905, the square, concrete-and-brick Port Reading Terminal building stood boldly on the Port Reading–Carteret Road, a bulwark of the company's strength and success.

Italian and Irish families joined together in 1904 to organize St. Anthony's Roman Catholic Church with Reverend Clement Carderelli of Perth Amboy as their advisor. John McNulty handled the finances for the congregation and arranged for the rental of a small building on Woodbridge Avenue to serve as a chapel.

By 1911, the congregation welcomed Father Columbino Galassi, pastor of the Holy Rosary Church in Perth Amboy, to oversee the Port Reading mission. Father Galassi initiated fund-raising projects to build a permanent church. Ten visiting priests and a crowd of over 800 people attended the laying of the cornerstone in June 1914. The church was consecrated on Sunday, October 25, 1914, a joyful day for the dedicated Catholics of Port Reading.

Other industries were drawn to Port Reading's desirable waterfront. They included the Koppers Company's plastic plant, built in 1959, and a Hess Oil Refinery in 1960. In 1961, Port Reading and Sewaren attempted to secede from the township of Woodbridge and incorporate as the Village of Warren. Both the separatists and their opponents offered various proposals and counter proposals, but ultimately the New Jersey Supreme Court upheld a lower court's decision that the two villages could not leave the township of Woodbridge.

In August 1963, the Woodbridge Redevelopment Agency announced plans for the "largest rehabilitation and conservation project up to that time in New Jersey," to take place in Port Reading.[5] Project Bowtie involved 328 buildings and covered an area of 106.4 acres that was shaped like a bowtie. S. Buddy Harris, executive director of the agency, headed the initiative, which was six years in the making. Much new construction took place, while outdated buildings were restored or torn down. School Number Nine was moved into a new residential development. A library, swimming pool, new firehouse, and an enlarged post office completed this huge undertaking.

SEWAREN

Two far-sighted gentlemen played significant roles in developing Sewaren in the later 1800s, New York philanthropist and president of the Central Railroad of New Jersey John Taylor Johnston, and local manufacturer and activist C.W. Boynton. In 1872, Johnston, a Plainfield resident, purchased approximately 300 acres along the shore of the Arthur Kill in East Woodbridge and made plans to develop the area into a healthful seaside vacation spot within easy access of northern and central New Jersey. Johnston and his family drafted the road plans and deeds from Old Road to the water's edge. Unfortunately, his dream was never fulfilled because of a financial downturn, but Johnston's son-in-law Robert DeForest built a grand summer hotel, The Sewaren House, in 1887. In its prime, the hotel, which was located south of Ferry Street on the beach side of Cliff Road, welcomed Thomas Alva Edison and President Grover Cleveland among its notable guests.

Also in 1877, Boynton opened his popular Boynton Beach resort on the waterfront not far from The Sewaren House. The complex featured a bathing beach with bathhouses, dance pavilion, pony rides, shooting gallery, nickelodeon, bowling alley, roller coaster, merry-go-round, a fleet of 100 row boats, and a restaurant complete with New York City chefs. He hired orchestras to play for dancing every Saturday night in the summer, affairs that found young and old dressed in their very best clothes. Boynton, who drank no alcoholic beverages, kept a strict watch over the decorum of his guests.

About the same time, Acker's Grove and Boat House opened nearby. Sunday school picnics were often held at Acker's, which also attracted boaters and fishermen. Henry Acker, the first of his family to settle in Sewaren, raised plants for seeds to supply the Peter Henderson Seed Company. The Ackers owned a

PORT READING COAL DUMPER, 1950. Using this dumper, the Reading Coal Company loaded barges with coal that arrived by train from out of state. (William Nevil)

canning factory in Sewaren that employed about 40 women to process locally grown tomatoes.

Excursion ferries, boats, trolleys, trains, bicycles, and finally the automobile brought the summer folk to Sewaren to enjoy the salt air, sand, and sparkling water. In 1892, Boynton purchased the steamboat *Pauline* to run each Tuesday and Saturday from Bayonne and Elizabethport to Sewaren. He knew that easy transportation to Boynton Beach was the key to success. The Jersey Central Railroad stopped at the Sewaren station, while the PRR brought vacationers as far as Woodbridge.

The Sewaren Land and Water Club, which was incorporated in 1892, provided the focus for the social life of Sewaren's permanent residents. Regattas, golf, card games, banquets, parties, and full-dress balls with dancing under the gaslights and stars filled the members' calendars. Boating activities also took place at the Sewaren Motor Boat Club on Smith's Creek.

The Sewaren House closed in 1913, and Boynton Beach shut down the next year. Both summer vacation spots became casualties of the "horseless carriage," which offered travelers a much wider choice of vacation possibilities. Boynton Beach was later sold to the Shell Oil Company.

Several suggestions have been offered concerning the origin of the name of Sewaren. Mr. Johnston may have honored a friend, S.E. Warren, by bestowing his name on the village. Or Mr. Boynton may have inadvertently named the community by hiring a Mr. Warren to work at Boynton Beach. Supposedly, a passenger alighting from a train at the Sewaren station who needed help was told to "See Warren." The question was repeated from one person to another, and somehow the railroad station became the Sewaren Station. Historian Dorothy Ludewig researched the archives for a possible Native American derivation but was unable to find any hopeful clues.

Mr. Johnston contributed the land for St. John's Episcopal Church, and Mr. Barrett of the Port Reading Coal Company presented the church with an authentic railroad bell for its tower. St. John's celebrated its 100th anniversary in 1992.

Writing in 1910, prominent Sewaren resident Helen Glidden Grant Tombs expressed the hope that "no spirit lurks in the marshes and that this 'Green Spot' may keep its freshness, and refresh the eye, for years to come." Sewaren may not have developed quite as Mrs. Tombs had hoped, but the village maintains its distinctive character today with its stately mansions along Cliff Road, a revitalized waterfront that has survived industrialization, and residents who take pride in preserving their community's unique physical features and historical heritage.

Though they share many common services, these separate communities that are included under the umbrella of Woodbridge Township have maintained distinct identities and neighborhoods. They have, however, remained relatively united in their common goals for the welfare of the township.

BOYNTON BEACH C. 1890. C.W. Boynton's resort complex in Sewaren was a popular summer spot until the automobile lured vacationers farther afield.

11. TWENTIETH-CENTURY PASSAGES: C. 1900–1950

War must be for the sake of peace, business for the sake of leisure, things necessary for the sake of things noble. —Aristotle, (from *Politics* VII, xiii)

In 1910, the Kingwood Athletic Association led fund-raising activities to erect a monument at the spot where Main Street intersects with Rahway Avenue to honor township veterans from all wars. Erected in 1911 and dedicated six years later, the Soldiers' and Sailors' Monument is inscribed, "In memory of the Soldiers and Sailors of Woodbridge, N.J., who fought in the wars of our Country." Little did the townsfolk know that in a short time the monument would also be honoring the men and women who served in World War I.

By 1924, the Memorial Municipal Building, commemorating the men who lost their lives in the Great War, was standing on property at the corner of Main Street and Rahway Avenue adjacent to the Soldiers' and Sailors' Monument. As with many initiatives, however, that involve the spending of public money, the time between the proposal of the idea to build a new town hall and a definite decision to proceed was slow and argumentative. Woodbridge had long outgrown its headquarters on School Street next to the firehouse. Town meetings were often so crowded that residents stood outside and listened through the windows, but years would pass before a new municipal building would be up and running.

A new town hall was first mentioned in the town minutes in 1914, and a public question concerning the issuing of bonds for the building brought the close vote of 376 yeas and 360 nays. Property owners offered sites for sale, but concerns with the flooding of Heard's Brook and other issues slowed the process. A bid was finally accepted and a contract awarded for a location in the center of town, which is now part of Woodbridge Park. But a November election intervened. The Democratic majority switched to a Republican majority in January 1918, and the project stalled. Contractors already hired demanded payment for materials purchased, and landowners again proposed other sites. The township committee temporarily tabled the plan.

One of the first orders of business after war was declared in 1917 was to assemble a Home Defense League. Colby Dill, E.H. Boynton, and Andrew Keyes organized the league, which enlisted most able-bodied men who were not serving in the armed forces. Members wore uniforms, carried firearms, and practiced drilling in preparation for an actual enemy attack. The town also formed a Comfort Committee, which held fairs and dances to raise funds for cigarettes to be sent to the troops.

When the war ended on November 11, 1918, the local government quickly voted funds for a town-wide celebration to be held the next day. Ruth Wolk reported that "Woodbridge, like the rest of the country, went wild." In the next few weeks, the township committee sent resolutions to the families of the servicemen who had died in battle: Antonio Coppola of Port Reading (who was the first man to lose his life), Lawrence Ballard, Stanley Carlson, Ira C. Dunn, Charles S. Farrell Jr., Edward M. Kelly, Stephen Kocsi, Charles Marty, Joseph Resh, William J. Senson, and Thomas Terp. The committee presented scrolls to all returning soldiers and sailors. The Comfort Committee, with added members William Coll, R. Valentine, Michael Holohan, and E.H. Boynton, was asked to investigate a permanent memorial for the deceased servicemen, while local veterans were welcomed home at an outdoor dinner held at the rear of the high school on Grove Avenue. The Woodbridge Field Club sponsored this lively affair.

The first post-war years found the United States enjoying a brief period of prosperity with rapid manufacturing expansion in the automobile, electrical appliance, chemical, and other industries. Americans were investing their savings in common stocks and buying freely on speculation. Woodbridge witnessed the growth of civic and women's organizations, the opening of a racing car track, and a new sense of cooperation among the movers and shakers who had disagreed for so long about the building of a new town hall. Residents were united in their quest to commemorate in some important and practical way the men who had died in the desperate battles of World War I. Without much hesitation, a memorial municipal building emerged as the perfect answer. A state law required that a minimum of $1,000 be raised before the project could begin. In 1919, 89 citizens made payments to finance the start of the building, and a committee composed of David A. Brown, John E. Breckenridge, Gorham L. Boynton, Arthur A. Overgaard, and E.L. Gridley was organized to supervise all details of site selection, design, and construction. J.K. Jensen, a local resident with an office on Main Street, was appointed the architect. The old town hall on School Street was later sold for $15 to the Woodbridge Fire Company next door.

After the building was well underway, a group known as the Mayor's Committee began preparations for a magnificent celebration to dedicate the new edifice. The committee selected Flag Day as the official dedication day to coincide with the 255th anniversary of Woodbridge Township. A long parade of officials, organizations, police forces, visiting firemen, floats, 13 bands, Gold Star Mothers, and many other marchers filled the gala morning, which was followed by a formal dedication ceremony. The Goodwill Band from Perth Amboy played the National Anthem while an enormous American flag was unfurled from the top of the new town hall, followed by hundreds of small flags that floated down over the crowd. Residents and visitors from near and far toured the building, participated in field

OFF TO WAR, APRIL 2, 1918. Woodbridge resident Edward M. Kelly (second from right in dark hat) and other county residents march off to serve in World War I. Kelly lost his life in France later that year. (Mary Ellen Grace Malague and Margaret Ann Grace Schoder)

events, competitions, and a block dance before gathering for a spectacular display of fireworks in the evening. A 96-page *Official Book of the 255th Anniversary and Memorial Celebration* and a souvenir medal are now collectors' items. The program book contained pictures of town personages and public buildings and alerted prospective home buyers to the amenities of Woodbridge:

> To those who are hearing the call of the suburbs, who long for the sane life of the country, and who are not familiar with the geographical location of Woodbridge, it may be set forth as lying in the North Eastern Section of New Jersey . . . and it is beyond one's power to imagine a community more favorably located. In no other place in New Jersey are there so many appealing factors that make the homeseeker pause and begin to build, in fancy, the mansion of his dreams.

Two days after the dedication, Mayor Louis Neuberg, a Republican (1924–1925), convened the first town meeting to be held in the new building. The Memorial Municipal Building survived for 70 years as a local landmark and the center of town government. Despite impassioned protests from townspeople, the building was demolished in 1994, and a large contemporary municipal hall and parking garage have taken its place. Older residents collected bricks from the fallen building to keep as mementos.

The American Legion started in town in the early 1920s. For many years Woodbridge Post No. 87 held its meetings in two rooms set aside for the Legion on the second floor of the town hall and later moved to its own building on Berry Street. The first officers included Barron L. McNulty, Roy E. Anderson, William Treen, Charles Kuhlman, August F. Greiner, George Hargis Prall, John C. Williams, and Stewart Schoder.

The Woman's Club of Woodbridge was founded in 1919 with Mrs. E.H. Boynton as the president. Among their many endeavors, the club sponsored a milk fund for school-age children and a student loan program, and purchased a portable iron lung for the Woodbridge Emergency Squad. In the 1940s, a Junior Woman's Club was organized that raised money for a U.S. Army field ambulance, and a Sub-Junior Woman's Club was started for high school girls. The organizations are no longer active in town.

Local men started the Rotary Club in 1923 as a branch of the International Rotary Club, which originated earlier in Chicago to develop high ethical standards among business and professional people serving the community. Since the founders scheduled meetings that rotated among the members' places of business, the club became known as the "Rotary Club." A few years later, the

A Parting Glimpse c. 1992. Woodbridge Historical Association members Frank LaPenta (left) and Robert J. McEwen, who both opposed the razing of the Memorial Municipal Building, discuss its imminent demise.

Lions Club came to town, a service organization known for its sponsorship of Youth Week, to enable students to experience the operation of local government. Grace Ellis Valentine organized the Janet Gage Chapter of the Daughters of the American Revolution (DAR) in 1924. The DAR is a society of women who can directly trace their ancestry to persons who fought for freedom in the Revolutionary War. In 1927, the chapter dedicated a large monument near the First Presbyterian Church with a plaque reading, "In memory of the Revolutionary Soldiers and Patriots of Woodbridge, New Jersey." Years later the monument was removed, but the plaque can be viewed today in the church cemetery. The chapter also presented an annual Good Citizen of the Year Award to a graduating high school girl. The Woodbridge DAR disbanded in the 1960s because of declining membership, with remaining members joining the Matochshoning Chapter in Metuchen. The Eunice Bloomfield Chapter of the Children of the American Revolution (CAR) was also active in town until the 1950s.

Election Day 1925 marked a Democratic victory, with William A. "Billy" Ryan chosen mayor. Ryan introduced a plan for a township park system and served on the executive committee to develop a sanitary sewer system linking Woodbridge and several Union County towns.

Beginning in 1927, cheering crowds packed "The World's Fastest Half-Mile Race Track," located off St. George's Avenue on the present site of Woodbridge High School. Car races were held every other Sunday from May through September. The course was originally constructed as a board track but was replaced in 1933 by an oiled dirt track because of the high cost of maintaining the wooden boards.

Without mufflers on the cars, the noise on racing days was often ear splitting and could be heard all the way to Main Street. Such cars as the Fronty Special and the Miller Majestic Special tore around the track in the best of times, but several famous drivers lost their lives at the speedway. By the mid-1930s, however, the Depression caused a decline in attendance, and although ticket prices were lowered and floodlights installed for night racing, the thrill-seeking spectators were simply not there anymore. The speedway closed after the 1938 season.

Early in 1928, Shell Eastern Petroleum Products, Inc. of Delaware announced plans to build a refinery in Sewaren. Amid strong opposition, especially from Sewaren homeowners, the township committee voted five to two to bring the company into Woodbridge. Although this industrial complex crowded the Sewaren waterfront with huge storage tanks and oil-refining equipment, Shell Oil also brought needed jobs to the area in the years to come.

One of the nation's first safety-engineered super highway intersections, known as the Woodbridge Cloverleaf, was constructed where U.S. Route 1 and New Jersey Route 35 converge. The New Jersey Department of Transportation has announced plans to extensively redesign the cloverleaf to alleviate major traffic congestion in the area, a project slated for completion in 2005.

On October 21, 1929, that fateful day of the Stock Market crash, the economic boom that had seemed such a sure thing to millions of Americans disappeared in a single day. Early in 1930, Mayor Ryan appointed a committee of citizens to study the effects of the mounting depression in town and to present their findings at a county meeting in New Brunswick. The Woodbridge Township Citizens' Committee for the Relief of the Unemployed and Needy began meeting in November 1931 with John E. Breckenridge as general chairperson. The township was especially devastated when the clay industry, long the backbone of Woodbridge's economic strength, collapsed. Another blow was struck when the First National Bank and Trust Company closed its doors in 1931 after a visit from the Federal Bank examiners. Only the Fords National Bank survived to serve Woodbridge patrons at the time. In 1932, the Civilian Conservation Corps (CCC), a national emergency relief program for young men, and a local work relief program to provide jobs for unemployed men to maintain the municipal parks were organized in town.

Ryan continued his efforts to stem the increasing unemployment and urged businesses and private citizens to purchase municipal bonds, known as "Baby Bonds," which were offered for sale in small denominations. Another citizens' group, the Woodbridge Township Taxpayers Association, emerged in 1932 and presented the township committee with a detailed list of measures to cut costs. John H. Love headed the three-day Woodbridge Township National Recovery Exposition, which took place at the Craftsmen's Club on Green Street late in 1933. A huge crowd viewed the array of exhibits displayed by businesses hoping to bolster their sales and services.

The Republicans moved back into power at the height of the Depression with the election of August F. Greiner as mayor in November 1933. Greiner would lead the township for the next 18 years. A World War I veteran and 32nd degree Mason, the new mayor owned and operated the Greiner Funeral Home on Green Street. On New Year's Day 1934, Mayor Greiner, familiarly known as Augie, presented his first message to the citizenry:

> Our road to recovery will not be an easy one and there will be many obstacles, chief among which will be the duty to meet debt obligations immediately in order that the public credit will not be impaired. We must make provision for payment of existing obligations in such a way as to cause the least embarrassment to the property owners of the Township as taxpayers. And while another administration is responsible for the condition, the duty will fall on this administration to provide the means for retirement of the debt. An absolute sacrifice and curtailment of improvements must therefore be insisted upon, at least until such time as general conditions adjust themselves.

The mayor told the taxpayers that if they paid their 1933 taxes in cash before the end of January, any interest owing would be waived. He also set in motion a plan for refinancing defaulted bonds and is credited with saving the town from bankruptcy.

"TUNES AND TOPICS OF 1935"

The Woman's Club sponsored a program of lighthearted music and skits in January 1935 at Woodbridge High School, an evening which must have provided a bright spot of laughter amid the grim throes of the Depression. The show featured songs by a group of local men and women calling themselves, "The Twitville Choral Society." Their hit of the evening was entitled, "Horsey, Keep Your Tail Up and Keep the Sun out of my Eyes," with Mrs. Clarence R. Davis as soloist. Costumes for this number were a "decided feature." Twelve township girls performed a specialty dance, "Gingham Day," while the Knights of Melody, led by "Tiny Tim," played for the show and for dancing afterward in the gym.

As president of the Mayors' Association of Middlesex County, Greiner recommended that public works contractors hire unemployed persons from within Woodbridge, rather than following the common practice of importing cheap labor. By the fall of 1935, new, local construction was making a slow comeback, and the list of area Works Progress Administration (WPA) employees was declining. Two years later a new Woodbridge National Bank, founded by

THE SPEEDWAY, MAY 28, 1933. From 1927 through 1938 crowds packed "The World's Fastest Half-Mile Race Track" off St. George's Avenue.

PACIFIC OFFENSIVE C. 1942. (Left to right): Corporal Lewis Niovich of Seanor, PA; Staff Sergeant Anthony Cavallero of Woodbridge; and Sec. Sergeant H. Hamm of Marietta, GA lie behind a log on Guadalcanal in the Solomon Islands. The Japanese were believed to be 50 yards away. (Anthony Cavallero)

Frank Van Syckle, opened, and the townsfolk began to look more optimistically toward the future.

The Woodbridge Emergency Squad was born on July 21, 1937, when a group of men at the Woodbridge Fire House formed a first aid organization. Elbur Richards, Gordon Hunt, Richard Larsen, Alfred W. Brown, and Elmer Vecsey served as the first officers. Other early members included Clifton Amos, William Roberts, Leo Menard, Alexander Hamilton, Joseph Quigley, Claude Gehman, John Orlick, Vincent Gray, Walter Housman, Charles Fisher, Eldon Raison, Leon Gerity, Raymond Olsen, Robert Heller, Julius Bernstein, Robert Leisen, Wilbur Jorgenson, Fred Zehrer Jr., and Peter Mooney. The all-volunteer squad started active duty on September 15, 1937, at six o'clock in the evening, using an emergency firetruck as an ambulance. Within a few weeks, the squad proved its value by quickly transporting two victims of a Fords explosion to the hospital.

The purchase of an ambulance headed the squad's wish list. Since Woodbridge had neither hospital nor a regulation emergency vehicle, badly injured or ill residents had to wait for the hospital itself to dispatch an ambulance to carry them, an arrangement which often caused the loss of vital time. The town's first ambulance arrived in February 1938. A month later, squad members quickly arrived at the scene of a fatal accident in Sewaren when a Central Railroad train crashed into a Shell Oil truck at West Avenue. By February 1, 1940, the squad had answered 415 calls, and in 1947, Mayor Greiner laid the cornerstone for the

Woodbridge Emergency Squad Building on Brook Street. Also in the 1940s, the squad received a citation from the Infantile Paralysis Division of the Jersey City Medical Center as the "most outstanding and efficient First Aid Squad in the State of New Jersey." The St. John's First Aid Squad from Fords organized in 1942, and the Avenel-Colonia Squad in 1945. All of the Woodbridge Township rescue squads have worked tirelessly through the years, responding to emergencies from childbirth to disastrous accidents, teaching first aid, and educating the public about health and safety issues.

The formation of the Woodbridge Alumni Golden Bears semi-professional football team in 1940 was another indication that the Depression was waning. Through the initial suggestion of board of education president Andrew P. Aaroe, the team provided young township men with the opportunity to play football after high school. By the end of the 1941 season, 18 players were members of the armed forces, including the team doctor, Henry A. Belafsky. Another ten members left for the war in 1942, and the team consolidated with their arch rivals, the Hopelawn Greyhounds. The Bears did not field teams again until 1945. In their 1946 program booklet, the Golden Bears included a special page remembering their players who were killed in World War II: James P. Lee, William J. Gill, Raymond F. Voelker, John B. Dunn Jr., Albert J. Leffler, William J. Finn, and Nathan H. Patten. The Bears played ball for 11 seasons and were considered one of the toughest semi-pro teams in New Jersey. Attendance at their games declined in the 1950s when college and professional football games became popular on television.

As the winds of war again swept across America, most of the demeaning consequences of the Depression finally disappeared. In February 1940, on the recommendation of Committeeman Herbert B. Rankin of Sewaren, the township committee unanimously passed a resolution endorsing the Moral Re-Armament Program, an international movement started in 1938 that was based on the concept that people can change the world by improving their own moral character. The committee received many congratulatory letters from organizations and individual citizens who endorsed the resolution.

By October 1940, local teachers serving as registrars had signed up 3,780 township men between 21 and 35 for selective military service. Walter Warr, Hampton Cutter, and James Crowley comprised the local draft board with Eugene Bird as clerk. Assistant Middlesex County Prosecutor James S. "Jimmer" Wight took the chairmanship of the Selective Service Advisory Board.

Woodbridge residents were stunned by an explosion on the morning of November 12, 1940, at the United Railway Signal Company in Port Reading. The company and a nearby Middlesex Water Company meter repair shop were demolished, while neighboring homes were severely damaged. Eight signal company workers were killed as well as water company foreman Dominick LaPenta. National newspapers announced that the company was sabotaged as part of a larger plot to damage American defense plants, but United Railway held no defense contracts at the time. No cause for the blast was ever found.

In February 1941, the township committee authorized a local Defense Council to coordinate with the New Jersey State Defense Council. (An even earlier Home Defense Program had been initiated in August 1940 following a directive from Governor A. Harry Moore.) Greiner and Rankin headed the council with township attorney Leon E. McElroy, Police Chief George E. Keating, and committee members completing the roster at that time. The council, however, did not move into action until five days after the Japanese attack on Pearl Harbor on December 7, 1941. Until that devastating moment in history, the town hoped and prayed that there would be no war. Woodbridge was divided into 16 zones based on the existing fire districts, and air raid sirens were installed.

Many residents answered the call to head or serve on the numerous committees and auxiliary services of the Defense Council. Residents volunteered as air raid wardens, messengers, couriers, drivers, and auxiliary firemen, while committees handled public information, medical services, rationing, first aid, blood drives, emergency road repair, surgical supplies, salvage drives, evacuation, demolition, bomb isolation and protection, decontamination, communications, public works, and lighting. In April 1942, the county held its first practice blackout with many additional, unannounced blackouts to follow.

The following May, Woodbridge's traditional Memorial Day Program was broadcast nationwide over radio station WOR with the town highlighted as a "Typical American Community." Speaking from the First Presbyterian Church Cemetery, Mayor Greiner stated that "a nation united is a strong nation . . . and we are ready to join our sister communities whenever called."

At first, the Defense Council handled the rationing of commodities for the community but as more items were placed on the list, a separate rationing board was appointed to oversee the distribution of tires, fuel oil, rubber footwear, gasoline, meat, sugar, butter, and canned goods. Charles E. Gregory, managing editor and later publisher of the *Independent-Leader*, headed the rationing board, which also supervised Carteret and Metuchen.

The members worked tirelessly and without compensation to handle the exceedingly difficult, seemingly thankless job of equitably distributing the many everyday items in short supply.

Letters formed a vital link between the homefront and the far-flung battlefields. Julia Ur of Second Street wrote hundreds of letters to her three sons and two brothers in the Army as well as to other local servicemen. Mrs. Ur, mother of 14 children, worked by day in the small arms shop of the Raritan Arsenal and wrote letters late into the evening. Sometimes she sent a brief greeting on a postcard; other times she would compose lengthy responses to the men's questions about what was happening at home. Her daughters helped her assemble her many replies into a scrapbook for posterity.

Marine Corporal Douglas M. Zenobia of Alice Place wrote a poignant poem about his buddy Martin J. Snee of Sewaren, who was killed in action on Guadalcanal on October 14, 1942. Excerpted here are several verses from his poem entitled "Including the Fourteenth:"

. . . Marty and I were together as usual
    On that perfect afternoon,
    Once more talking of home
    And that we would be there soon.

We said so long that evening
    As we always did before,
    But little did we know that things
    Weren't scheduled that way anymore.

. . . The fellow in front of me
    Turned around and said
    Doug, I hate like hell to say this
    But your buddy Marty is dead.

. . . My thoughts were back in Jersey
    (Funny but it's true)
    Of what we used to talk about
    And of things we would do.

Well, Marty, you are gone now
    And those things we'll never do
    But fella, you have my promise
    That I'll even it up for you.

VICTORY SHIP C. 1945. Designed for post-war operation, the Woodbridge Victory *was launched in 1945. (Ray J. Schneider)*

Army infantryman James "Dubs" Gerity described his D-Day experiences (June 5, 1944) in a letter to his brother David, which was published in the *Independent-Leader*:

> After leaving England, we were taken down and loaded on a LCI [Landing Craft Infantry] and spent four days on it waiting for the bell to ring for the first round in the main event. . . . We moved around a bit but stayed close to shore until the morning of D-Day when we moved across and waited off the other shore until our time to land. . . . Then about 6 PM, it was our turn and we headed in. After the LCI went in as far as it could we got off that and into a small craft which we thought would take us right in. Much to our dismay, it stopped a couple of hundred yards from shore and let down its front for us to disembark . . . into water almost neck-deep . . . And while we were making our way in, old Herman the German dropped a couple of his now well-known 88's along the beach, which didn't exactly serve to cheer us up any. . . .We were also bothered quite a bit by snipers who had stayed behind to raise some mischief of their own. And, of course, their artillery—usually those 88's also had to be contended with . . .

On Mother's Day in 1944, the Honor Roll plaque listing the names of all local servicemen and women was unveiled on School Street in Woodbridge Park. Mrs. Harry Stankiewicz, the mother of U.S. Marine Robert J. Madden, the first man from Woodbridge proper to be killed in action, dedicated the monument.

The American Red Cross established a permanent headquarters on Main Street in 1944 with a long list of volunteers, both male and female. That same year the organization collected $21,500, which far exceeded their goal. Mary Jane Rothfuss organized the Camp Kilmer Council of the Red Cross to provide needed items for the camp, which was located in Raritan (now Edison) Township and for the men of the anti-aircraft unit stationed on Strawberry Hill.

The 45th victory ship to be built at the Bethlehem Fairfield Shipyard in Baltimore, Maryland, honored Woodbridge Township. Designed for post-war operation, the *Woodbridge Victory* was launched early in 1945. Local officials contributed a plaque outlining the history of the township and books for the ship's library.

In a type setting 4 inches high, the *Independent-Leader* announced in an extra edition on May 7, 1945, "GERMANY FOLDS UP." The accompanying front-page story stated that "one phase of the global struggle between the forces of democracy and fascism ended in victory . . . Into this gigantic struggle Woodbridge Township alone put nearly 3,500 men and women." Ruth Wolk reported that there were no local celebrations on V-E Day. Residents' concerns centered on the fighting men in the Pacific area, and they spent a quiet day in their crowded churches and synagogues. The *Independent-Leader* again published an extra edition on August 14, 1945, with the simple headline, "WAR ENDS." Houses of worship were filled, but so were the streets all over town. Cars decorated with bunting and flags streamed around town until three o'clock in the morning. On a directive from the state police, Chief George E. Keating closed all liquor stores at nine o'clock that night with orders not to re-open until noon the following day.

Mayor Greiner appointed a large committee headed by Mr. Gregory to arrange a welcome-home celebration for returning veterans to take place on Sunday, October 29, 1946. Led by guest of honor General George K. Nold, a hero of Okinawa, more than 4,000 marchers participated in a parade that started at Legion Stadium in the Fulton Street area and concluded at the newly erected Veterans' Memorial in Woodbridge Park. Thirty thousand people crowded the streets to pay tribute to all those who had fought for their country. Judges for the band performances and the floats watched the parade from a reviewing stand on Main Street. A brief, solemn ceremony followed the parade in front of the Veterans' Memorial, which listed the names of all those men who gave their lives in both world wars. Afterward, the Gold Star families were honored guests at a reception at the Colonia home of Mrs. Edward K. Cone. During the war, people throughout the United States displayed service flags in their front windows to honor family members serving their country. A blue star represented each person in service, while a silver star indicated a wounded serviceman and a gold star stood for those who were killed in action.

HOMECOMING, OCTOBER 29, 1946. A triumphant parade along Main Street welcomed home the returning veterans of World War II.

THE GOLDEN BEARS C. 1948. Woodbridge's own semi-pro football team was active for 11 seasons in the 1940s and 1950s.

Mr. Gregory composed the words inscribed on the Veterans' Memorial Monument:

> These men died defending the incorruptible ideals and the God-fearing obedience of the world's greatest symbol of freedom for all men—the United States of America. From this community, deeply rooted in the proud tradition of a nation's devotion to the true principles of equality, justice and honor, these sons marched forth inspired and unafraid. They gave their lives that our cherished citadel of liberty could stand unblemished. May that peace which passeth all understanding be with them throughout eternity.

The Woodbridge Housing Authority, under Mayor Greiner's guidance, provided emergency, short-term housing for veterans and their families. Woodbridge also received a state grant for 50 temporary homes in Port Reading. These temporary dwellings filled a crucial housing need for ten years.

Two additional organizations started in town shortly after the war. Memorial Post 4410 of the Veterans of Foreign Wars began with 94 charter members and the Kiwanis Club with 26 members. Both groups, together with the VFW Auxiliary, have made many valuable contributions to the community.

Township citizens bravely answered the call to serve their country twice during the first half of the twentieth century and joined together to support each other during the years of the Great Depression. Now Woodbridge looked ahead to a time for celebrating its own long history and heritage, New Jersey's 300th Anniversary and the Bicentennial of the United States, as well as witnessing a surge of new commercial buildings, a regional shopping mall, and many new private homes, condominiums, and apartment houses.

"HAIL, HAIL, THE GANG'S ALL HERE" c. 1950. With Mayor Augie Greiner (center) at the piano, a group of township movers and shakers gathers for a song at the Log Cabin on St. George's Avenue (left to right): Mr. Fitz Patrick, Log Cabin owner Lou Horner, unidentified, Hugh B. Quigley (who succeeded Greiner as mayor), unidentified, Greiner, former mayor John Breckenridge, Superintendent of Schools Victor C. Nicklas, unidentified, and local dentist Dr. Barrett.

12. TWENTIETH-CENTURY PASSAGES: 1951–2002

Let the great world spin for ever down the ringing grooves of change. —Alfred Lord Tennyson (from "Locksley Hall")

It was almost supper time on the cold, gray Tuesday afternoon of February 6, 1951. Suddenly, three young teenagers who were skating at a local watering hole at the intersection of the PRR and Reading Railroad tracks and Edgar Hill Station heard a fast train approaching. As it whizzed by, David Maher and Walt Housman Jr., of Bucknell Avenue, and Richie Anderson of Hillside Avenue, were surprised to see their bicycles, which were parked on a nearby hill, knocked to the ground by the force of the passing train. The boys quickly changed to their shoes and ran to inspect the bikes, which appeared to be in good shape. Cold and hungry, they headed home.

When they stopped at the Housmans' home to say their goodbyes, Mrs. Housman told them that Walt's father had just rushed off to the Woodbridge Emergency Squad headquarters because of a train accident downtown. Walt, Dave, and Richie looked at one another in shocked recognition. They knew exactly which train had crashed. They had no way of knowing, however, that this train wreck would be the fifth deadliest railroad accident in the nation's history.

It was standing room only on the PRR's commuter train, No. 733, when it left Exchange Place, Jersey City, at 5:10 p.m. with more than 900 passengers en route to the Jersey Shore. Striking switchmen had forced many more travelers onto the *Broker*, named for its commuters who worked on Wall Street. The train, which was not scheduled to stop in Woodbridge, crashed at 5:43 p.m. as it crossed a temporary wooden trestle at the Legion Place overpass just beyond the station. The trestle had been placed at this point to allow New Jersey Turnpike construction employees to work on the main track. Eighty-five people were killed and 345 injured.

The train was traveling at 50 m.p.h. in an area where the speed had been reduced to 25 m.p.h. at 1 p.m. that day. Several trains had safely passed over the trestle earlier in the afternoon. Prior to departure, the train's crew had reviewed the speed reduction instructions, but the railroad did not require warning signals or lights on the tracks when "slow orders" were published in advance. The weight of the 320,000-pound locomotive caused the rails to shift, initiating the derailment. The engine tender (coal car) and 8 of the *Broker's* 11 cars went off the tracks with the third and fourth coaches containing most of the deaths.

The majority of the victims were taken to Perth Amboy General Hospital (now the Raritan Bay Medical Center), where doctors, nurses, and other hospital employees worked tirelessly to administer to the injured. Woodbridge residents, especially those living in the Fulton Street area, immediately came to the rescue of the less seriously injured passengers by helping them to contact their families and offering food, clothing, and transportation home.

The Interstate Commerce Commission announced on April 19, 1951 that "Excessive speed on a curve of a temporary track" caused the accident. At first, the engineer Joseph Fitzsimmons of Rahway stated that he had complied with the 25 m.p.h. directive but later admitted that he was waiting to see the caution lights on the tracks before slowing down. Fitzsimmons continued working for the railroad until his retirement in 1953, but he never drove another train. The PRR settled out of court with all plaintiffs for an undisclosed amount of money and made improvements totaling $12 million to its signal systems.

Woodbridge resident Captain Henrik (Kurt) Carlsen, a merchant seaman and native of Denmark, found himself in a desperate situation in late December 1951. His freighter the *Flying Enterprise* had been badly damaged in a storm in the North Atlantic, and as Carlsen struggled to keep his ship afloat, an enormous wave smashed broadside, causing the hull to crack on each side and across the deck

FATAL ACCIDENT. One of the deadliest train wrecks in U.S. history occurred in Woodbridge on February 6, 1951.

amidships. An urgent SOS brought help when the vessel could no longer be steered. On December 31, Carlsen arranged for the rescue of his 40 crewmen and 10 passengers 320 miles off the English coast. Carlsen stayed on board his stricken ship alone for the next five days, while a tugboat pulled it toward Falmouth.

On January 4, a seaman from a rescue ship made a daring leap onto the *Flying Enterprise* to help the captain, but when they were only 41 miles from shore, another violent storm cut the tow line. All hope to save the ship was now lost. On January 10, when the freighter was nearly flat on her side, the two men jumped into the ocean and were swiftly rescued. Forty minutes later the *Flying Enterprise* sank.

Carlsen was commended by President Harry S. Truman and King Frederick IX of Denmark. After a ticker-tape parade in New York City on January 17, he was honored two days later at a huge hometown parade on Main Street, which was attended by New Jersey Governor Alfred E. Driscoll. When Mayor Hugh B. Quigley presented Carlsen with a key to the town, Quigley stated, "We are proud that you, a man of courage, a man unafraid, selected Woodbridge for your home." Carlsen continued to sail the seas for the American Export-Isbrandtsen Lines, retiring in 1976. He lived in town until his death in 1990 at the age of 75.

A few months later, the perennially popular Mayor Greiner announced that he would not seek another term, and in 1952 he was named "Citizen of the Year" by the township committee. Many new enterprises arrived in town during the administration of Mayor Quigley (1952–1959), a Democrat, who took office in January 1952. The Elizabethtown Gas Company purchased land in Iselin for a distribution center, Ronson Corporation International opened offices and a warehouse on U.S. Route 1, the U.S. Department of Defense released $338,000 in federal funds for the construction of a new Army National Guard Armory on outer Main Street, and the Public Service Corporation announced plans to expand its Sewaren generating plant.

The early 1950s marked the beginning of changes in the structure of the township committee. The township form of government had originally evolved from a local law of 1798, which introduced the committee as the community's elected body of officials. In even earlier times, however, when Woodbridge was a sparsely populated village, major decisions were made at an annual town meeting of all qualified voters. As the nineteenth century progressed and local affairs became more complex, the township committee gradually replaced the town meeting as the governing body. Until 1917, however, a vote at the annual town meeting was still required to levy taxes.

The pre–Revolutionary War slogan "No taxation without representation" took on new meaning in Colonia in the 1950s and ultimately brought about a reorganization of the town government. At the time, Woodbridge Township was divided into three wards: Ward One (Woodbridge proper), Ward Two (Colonia, Fords, Hopelawn, Iselin, and Keasbey), and Ward Three (Avenel, Port Reading, and Sewaren) with seven committeemen. Colonia had grown to a voting population of 6,000 but had no representatives of its own in the town government. The committeemen from Ward Two lived in Fords and Iselin, leaving Colonia on the "receiving end of a complete shutout."[1]

Led by John Evanko, several community organizations of Colonia united in 1957 as the Council of Civic Associations to consolidate efforts to bring representation and needed improvements to that part of town. Their endeavors paid off the following year when the township committee formed Ward Four (Iselin) and Ward Five (Colonia). Running as Republicans, Evanko and David T. Miller Sr. were elected as the first committeemen from Colonia.

The decade of the 1960s brought other major changes in the town government. In 1961, Mayor Frederick M. Adams and the township committee recommended a charter study that would review the entire operation of the local government. The electorate overwhelmingly approved the Charter Study Referendum and chose Donald Barnickel, Mary P. Connolly, Edward P. Keating, Christian Stochel, and Dr. H. Kenneth Staffin to serve on the commission. Following a nine-month examination, the commission recommended a strong mayor-council form of government. The voters agreed.

Under this plan as set forth in the Faulkner Act, the mayor would serve as chief executive. (The New Jersey Optional Municipal Charter Law, popularly known as the Faulkner Act, was passed in 1950, and it recommended four possible forms of government that municipalities might adopt.) The mayor-council plan would

GLORIOUS HOMECOMING, JANUARY 1952. Woodbridge resident Captain Kurt Carlsen was honored with a parade and ceremony after his heroic efforts to save his sinking merchant ship in the North Atlantic. Carlsen is shown here with his daughter Sonia and wife Agnes on the steps of the Memorial Municipal Building. (Karen Carlsen Mueller and Sonia Carlsen Fedak)

alleviate the feelings of sectionalism that had often dominated the operation of the government in past years. The mayor and council members would be elected for terms of four years, with other officers and a business administrator appointed by the mayor. With the executive and legislative functions now separated, the council would have complete flexibility to establish departments that would most efficiently serve the residents. The mayor would be responsible for the execution and administration of the policies of the township, while the council would establish these policies. The mayor-council plan became effective on January 1, 1964, during the administration of Walter Zirpolo (1962–1967).

The 1960s also brought the New Jersey Shakespeare Festival to town, state, and local tercentenary celebrations, national honors to Woodbridge, and the introduction of the major land-use concept that would transform the disused clay banks into Woodbridge Center.

The New Jersey Shakespeare Festival opened in the summer of 1961 with actress and producer Rose Belafsky as the executive director. Their first production was *As You Like It*, which was dramatized on an outdoor grassy stage. At that time, New York City was the only other place producing Shakespeare's plays out of doors and free of charge. The festival is no longer in existence.

Township historian Ruth Wolk was appointed chairperson of a committee to organize local events to honor New Jersey's Tercentenary (1664-1964). On New Year's Day of 1964, the National Guard raised American and Tercentenary flags at the town hall to recognize New Jersey's 300th anniversary as well as to inaugurate the new municipal form of government. Miss Wolk directed an afternoon program that day that traced the early European settlements in New Jersey. The festivities concluded with the presentation of a four-tiered birthday cake topped by the figure "300."

In April 1964, Woodbridge was selected as one of ten municipalities in the nation to receive the highly prized "All-America City" Award. The Woodbridge Business and Professional Women (BPW), a club organized locally in 1957, and the Junior Chamber of Commerce (Jaycees) sponsored the community in 1963 in a competition conducted by *Look* magazine and the National Municipal League. After Woodbridge was judged a semi-finalist in November of that year, Miss Wolk, who represented the BPW, and Jaycee member S. Buddy Harris presented the credentials of the township to the All-America Cities' jury in Detroit. Dr. George Gallup of the nationally known Gallup Poll headed the jury. The following March, Woodbridge welcomed the exciting news that the community had placed among the top ten winners because of the progress made by Woodbridge and its forward-looking governmental operations. The town held two special events in April 1964: the raising of the All-America City flag at the Memorial Municipal Building and a grand dinner-dance at the National Guard Armory.

Woodbridge was in the spotlight again in 1967. Joseph M. Racina, chairman of the Woodbridge Citizens' Advisory Committee, directed the town's successful efforts in the National Home and Community Beautification Contest. The township was selected as one of eleven communities in the nation to receive trophies for the best short-term clean-up campaigns.

The year 1969, the 300th anniversary of the granting of the original charter to the township of Woodbridge in 1669, was a time of continuous celebration, starting on the first day of the year. After the township flag was raised, Mayor Ralph P. Barone and his family rode in a vintage stagecoach to St. Anthony's Auditorium in Port Reading for a reception. In February, the schools joined the festivities with tercentenary projects in every classroom. Local organizations presented historical programs in March. "George Washington" and "Janet Gage" returned to town on Memorial Day to reenact their patriotic activities. Elizabeth V. Novak of Fords portrayed Janet Gage, while Gary Morton, a WHS student, played the part of her servant, Joe.

Dark clouds and showers on a June weekend did not deter the crowds from attending a traditional country fair in Merrill Park, now a county park in Iselin, where almost every organization and business was represented. Fireworks,

HONORING TOWNSHIP AND STATE. *January 1, 1964 ushered in the 300th anniversary celebration for New Jersey and Woodbridge. (Left to right): S. Buddy Harris, director of the Woodbridge Redevelopment Corporation; Mayor Walter Zirpolo; and Tercentenary chairperson Ruth Wolk. (Ruth Wolk)*

famous bands, Broadway and television acts, and favorite picnic foods combined to make a memorable Fourth of July jubilee. These major fetes were interspersed with smaller affairs, including drum and bugle competitions, concerts by the Lafayette College Glee Club and the U.S. Marine Corps Band, as well as church and synagogue services. Monuments were unveiled honoring the first printer, James Parker, in his family's plot in the Presbyterian churchyard and the first miller, Jonathan Dunham, at the Trinity Episcopal Church. The tercentenary events culminated on November 15 with the grand and glorious 300th Anniversary Ball.

In 1960, Mayor Adams created the Woodbridge Redevelopment Agency to investigate possible community renewal projects in various areas of town. Under the leadership of its executive director, S. Buddy Harris, and its chairman, Father William H. Payne, the agency hired Victor Gruen Associates of New York City to present detailed proposals. The Gruen Report recommended that the abandoned clay banks in the vicinity of upper Main Street be transformed into a vast shopping mall and related enterprises. Until that time the clay area had been considered an unusable wasteland. The report also made revitalization proposals for other sections of the township. The Redevelopment Agency and Gruen Associates named their revolutionary proposal: "Woodbridge Tomorrow."

Township officials were disappointed to learn that no federal or state money was available, but the Redevelopment Agency went ahead and requested the Gruen firm to follow up with a more detailed study entitled the "Conceptual Core Plan." This 1963 Gruen Report envisioned a complete, modern urban center. During the next year the Alexander Summer Appraisal Company of Newark used the Gruen Report to recommend the addition of municipal and residential buildings to the regional shopping mall. Now the initiative was known by the all-encompassing name of "Centrosphere."

The Gruen and Summer Reports brought Woodbridge into the national spotlight with major magazines and trade journals reporting on the varied possibilities for improvement in an abandoned clay mining area. By this time, Mayor Walter Zirpolo had taken office and was interviewing possible developers, a search that lasted three years. In late 1966, Federated Department Stores of New York City and the Rouse Company of Baltimore, Maryland, were ready to combine forces to handle the project. Connecticut General Life Insurance Company of Hartford, Connecticut, later joined the team.

In 1967, Democrat Ralph P. Barone was appointed mayor to complete the unexpired term of Mayor Zirpolo, who had resigned. While continuing the planning for Woodbridge Center, Mayor Barone declared, "It's the most exciting development in the history of Woodbridge." Land clearance for the immense $15 million project to be situated on a 135-acre site between U.S. Route One, State Route Nine, and Metuchen Avenue commenced in 1968.

Woodbridge Center, one of the largest two-level enclosed shopping malls in the East, opened in 1970 with five large department stores: Abraham and Straus, Steinbach's, Stern's, Hahne's, and J.C. Penney. In the initial planning stages of the

Center, a municipal office complex, a hospital, high-rise apartments, the public library, theaters, and a community park complete with band shell, tennis courts, playing fields, and a lake created from a large clay pit were included in the project but none materialized. In 2002, Woodbridge Center defines itself on its website as a "family-oriented shopping center." Macy's, Lord and Taylor, Fortunoff's, J.C. Penney, and Sears are joined by over 200 specialty stores, 14 sit-down restaurants, 15 snack places, and a retail program in the common areas. The Center sponsors a Mall Walkers Club and events for children.

Major building projects continued during the administration of Republican mayor John J. Cassidy (1972–1979). Woodbridge Center was enlarged, and the Woodbridge Center Office Complex, the Prudential Plaza Office Complex, and a senior citizens' building on Rahway Avenue dedicated to the late Mayor Adams were completed. The new Woodbridge Public Library opened in 1975 with eight branches at that time. Several branches were closed in later years with Fords, Iselin, and the Henry Inman Library in Colonia continuing in use. The Sewaren Library remains in operation as an independent facility.

Mayor Cassidy also instituted the first injunction against New York City for polluting the Sewaren waterfront with garbage and hospital refuse. The injunction resulted in the city assuming full monetary responsibility for the cleanup of the beaches. And Mayor Cassidy can also take credit for helping to establish the annual St. Patrick's Day Parade.

DEBUTANTES, 1966. Joanne Santore (left) served as chairperson of the sixth annual Debutante Ball sponsored by the Business and Professional Women's Club with Linda Harned (right) as vice chairperson. (William Harned)

ACHIEVEMENT TROPHY, 1967. Joseph M. Racina (second from left), who spearheaded the township's Clean-Up, Fix-Up and Paint-Up campaign; and Congressman Edward J. Patton (second from right) proudly hold the Achievement Award won by Woodbridge in the National Home and Community Beautification Contest. (Joseph M. Racina)

In 1971, the Woodbridge Metropark railroad station opened in Iselin. Metropark provided a major stop for the Amtrak Metroliners traveling from Boston to Washington and also for New Jersey Transit trains to Newark and Penn Station, New York. In 2002, Metropark holds the record as the third-busiest railroad station in New Jersey, outdistanced only by Newark and Hoboken. More than 6,000 people pass through Metropark each day.

Joseph Somers headed the United States Bicentennial (1776–1976) Committee in town. The local celebration centered around the construction and dedication of a replica of James Parker's print shop. Located in an area of Rahway Avenue designated as Bicentennial Park, the print shop was built from beams and boards taken from the remnants of a 200-year old barn situated on a county-owned tract in South Brunswick. An eighteenth-century vintage printing press was installed inside the shop. The Parker Print Shop is no longer open to the public, but the township committee is considering new uses for the building.

Mayor Joseph DeMarino (1980–1983), a Democrat, served on the bond-issuing committee to reconstruct the Green Street Circle, a project that was finally completed after years of tragic accidents at the site. Mayor DeMarino also continued the town's fight against the filling of liquid natural gas tanks on Staten

Island, a protracted controversy with the Federal Energy Regulatory Commission, which finally ended with the withdrawal of the application to fill the tanks.

Philip M. Cerria, a Republican, succeeded Mayor DeMarino in 1984 and placed environmental planning at the top of his priority list. He also persuaded the State Department of Corrections to place hard-core inmates at the East Jersey State Prison in Avenel behind maximum-security walls and to require them to wear uniforms 24 hours a day.

Democrat James E. McGreevey was elected mayor in November 1991 and was returned to office in 1995 and 1999. Prior to becoming mayor, McGreevey, a native of Carteret, served as a member of the New Jersey General Assembly from 1990 to 1992. While mayor, he was also elected to the state senate in 1993 to represent the 19th Legislative District (Middlesex County). In November 2001, McGreevey was elected the 51st governor of New Jersey, and stepped down as mayor the following January. At that time Councilwoman Brenda Velasco became the first woman mayor of Woodbridge. Her term of office lasted only two days during an interim change before Councilman Frank Pelzman was selected the 20th mayor on January 17, 2002.

Mayor McGreevey supervised an annual township budget of approximately $70 million and a workforce of some 850 municipal employees. His administration

FROM MAYOR TO GOVERNOR. *After serving as mayor of Woodbridge Township from 1991 to 2001, James E. McGreevey was elected governor of New Jersey. (Office of the Governor)*

established the Woodbridge Economic Development Corporation to bring new jobs and investments to the community and initiated efforts to revitalize the downtown business district.

On November 8, 1998, a Medal of Honor permanent memorial was dedicated at Veterans' Park on St. George's Avenue to honor Woodbridge's two winners of the nation's highest award. The Medal of Honor is awarded in the name of Congress to a person who distinguishes himself or herself by gallantry or intrepidity at the risk of life above and beyond the call of duty while engaged in an action against any enemy of the United States or while engaged in military combat against a foreign force. On March 8, 1968, while serving with MACV forces in Kien Phong Province of the Republic of Vietnam, First Lieutenant Jack J. Jacobs distinguished himself by saving an Allied company of the Second Battalion, 16th Infantry, Ninth Infantry Division from being overrun and destroyed by a Viet Cong battalion. Though wounded, he took command of the unit, re-established its fighting effectiveness, repeatedly crawled through fire-swept paddies to rescue 14 wounded, and single-handedly killed 3 of the enemy.

Carl E. Petersen was honored posthumously. At the age of 25, Petersen, a trained civilian machinist's mate, distinguished himself when he repaired a rusted and split gun and fired upon Boxer rebels during the Boxer Rebellion in China in 1900. The Boxers were a secret society of strongly nationalistic Chinese who

ABOVE AND BEYOND THE CALL OF DUTY C. 1970. Woodbridge resident First Lieutenant Jack H. Jacobs (second from right) was awarded the Medal of Honor by President Richard M. Nixon for saving an allied company of the 9th Infantry Division from being destroyed by a Viet Cong battalion on March 8, 1968. (Jack H. Jacobs)

attacked the foreign legations of Peking and killed 300 people. While he was aboard the U.S.S. *Newark* off the coast of China during the siege, an emergency inside the city created the immediate need for a machinist. Alone, Petersen boarded a train and arrived outside the gates of the city, where he hid for three days in a forest before penetrating enemy siege lines and entering the city. He was wounded twice but survived the Boxer Rebellion and later lived in Avenel for 53 years until his death at the age of 96.

As Woodbridge approaches its 335th birthday, the township still stands at the crossroads of central New Jersey, but today the sparsely populated farming village of 1669 has been transformed into the sixth-largest municipality in New Jersey. More than 97,000 people make their homes in Woodbridge Township, which is the hub of major railroads and highways leading in all directions.

For more than a century, the clay industry enlarged and diversified the population and provided the community with a strong economic base. Clay has been replaced by the headquarters of many national and international companies, an immense shopping mall, various smaller industries, and a thriving waterfront. And as evidenced by statements in the 1990 Master Plan, Woodbridge is committed to preserving residential neighborhoods and balancing land uses. The town is included in the U.S. Department of Environmental Protection's Metropolitan Watershed (Watershed Management Area Number Seven), a 180-square-mile section of New Jersey that includes parts of Middlesex, Hudson, Essex, and Union Counties, the Elizabeth, Rahway, and Woodbridge Rivers, the Arthur Kill, and Newark Bay. The Metropolitan Watershed is striving to prevent further pollution and to educate the public to its responsibility to keep these waterways healthful and safe for both the people and the many animals and plants that are all integral parts of this vital land and water area.

A local environmental organization, Riverwatch, started about 1995 and its members, all volunteers, have been involved since that time with maintaining the cleanliness of the area waterways. Former New Jersey assemblyman and Woodbridge Township committee member Ernie Oros was among the founders of the group.

As its motto states, "Giving the past a future" is the primary goal of the Historical Association of Woodbridge Township. The organization is growing in membership with plans for active participation in the preservation of the town's historical sites. Several members have published books on various aspects of Woodbridge's heritage, while other publications are in the making. The association is developing local historical information to be added to the schools' curriculums, not only to fulfill the new state requirement to teach local history, but also to guarantee that future township students are provided with a firm foundation in the long and vibrant history of Woodbridge. As Martha J. Morrow, beloved social sciences teacher at WHS, stated in the late 1960s:

> A spirit of local patriotism is vital to the survival of a democracy. Local
> patriotism is nurtured by a knowledge of the origin and meaning of our

local institutions and affairs . . . and since we need to know where we have been if we are to know where we are going, we must rely upon written records of local lore and personal memoirs.[2]

Writing in the 1870s about the founding years of Woodbridge through the Revolutionary War, Reverend Joseph W. Dally concluded that the town "was once a much more conspicuous and important place than it now is." Dally feared that selfishness and a lack of public spiritedness and morality would prevent the continued development of Woodbridge and the country as well . . . "and as many young eyes may glance over these pages we cannot close without this gently-spoken warning: *Beware of the ship-wreck!*"[3]

Leon E. McElroy, who continued the township's history after the Revolutionary War, might not agree with Dally's concerns for the future, but he writes without enthusiasm about the contributions of the local citizens during its second 100 years:

> The story of Woodbridge in the 19th century can well parallel the advancement made in the progress of our infant nation; not that it was by virtue of such advancement destined to greatness, but that it kept pace with the times even though the contributions of its citizens were meager.[4]

VETERANS' MEMORIALS, 2002. The monument at left, a memorial to veterans who died in World Wars I and II, originally stood in Woodbridge Park and was later moved to the George Frederick Plaza off St. George's Avenue. The monuments on the right honor veterans from the Korean and Vietnam wars. (Ray J. Schneider)

And Amy Edgar Breckenridge, who authored a booklet in 1945 entitled *Disappearing Landmarks of Woodbridge*, expressed a feeling of loss about times past:

> With the passing of the landmarks, the social customs and habits of a community change. Gone is the simplicity of former times. We have no more the unconventional gatherings such as apple bees, husking frolics and quilting parties. We do not wish the old times back, but if the genial spirit of that time could be restored, we might be better for it. If our forefathers should come back today, they would find very little to remind them of the Old Woodbridge of nearly three hundred years ago.[5]

In the 1960s, however, Dorothy Ludewig and Ruth Wolk looked with optimism toward the future of the township. Mrs. Ludewig believed that Woodbridge "is attuned to the pulse of the twentieth century. With our roots richly nourished by yesterday's experiences plus a serious commitment toward the protection of our environment in the present, a promising future is inevitable."[6] Miss Wolk wished that she "could come back here 100 years from now and see all the growth, progress and miracles that science will come up with to make Woodbridge Township an outstanding community."[7]

As Mrs. Breckenridge pointed out, it is true that those first, intrepid English settlers would not recognize much of Woodbridge today, but if they persisted in their search, they might take comfort in knowing that Jonathan Dunham's millstone and his remodeled homestead still exist. They would also be heartened to see familiar names on the ancient gravestones of the First Presbyterian and Trinity Churches' cemeteries and realize that the first dusty roads they traveled on are still major streets in town: Main Street, Rahway Avenue, and Amboy Avenue. Colonists arriving a few years later would remember the Cross Keys Tavern, which has not changed drastically since playing its role in Woodbridge history and may yet be returned to its former importance.

But these first fathers and mothers would also find something more important than landmarks. They would surely sense a similar spirit of dedication and community among the diverse citizenry of contemporary Woodbridge. To be sure, they may encounter other languages being spoken, but they would meet people striving for ever-improving schools, safe neighborhoods, clean waterways, and rewarding lives for themselves and their children. These folks stepping out of the past would soon realize that their counterparts today are reflecting the same basic democratic values and ideals that led the Bloomfields, Dunhams, Moores, Dennises, Pikes, and all the other founding families to Woodbridge in the first place.

ENDNOTES

Information quoted from Leon E. McElroy is credited to him within the text. His complete history was published in the *Atom Tabloid* in 1958, but the page numbers and exact dates are unclear. McElroy wrote extensively about nineteenth-century water and rail transportation in the Middlesex County area in his history of Woodbridge Township during the nineteenth and early twentieth centuries.

The full text of the "Charter Granted to the Towne of Woodbridge on June 1st, 1669" can be found in Reverend Joseph W. Dally's *Woodbridge and Vicinity, The Story of a New Jersey Township*.

CHAPTER ONE

1. Gallagher, William B. *When Dinosaurs Roamed New Jersey*. pp. 67–68.
2. Ibid., pp. 68–69.
3. Baird, Donald. "Medial Cretaceous Carnivorous Dinosaur and Footprints from New Jersey." *The Mosasaur: The Journal of the Delaware Valley Paleontological Society*, October, 1989. pp. 60–61.
4. Clayton, W. Woodford, ed. *History of Union and Middlesex Counties, New Jersey*. p. 552.
5. Dally, Reverend Joseph W. *Woodbridge and Vicinity: The Story of a New Jersey Township*. p. 31.
6. Gilman, C. Malcolm B. *The Story of the Jersey Blues*. pp. 89–91.
7. Ibid. p. 91.

CHAPTER TWO

1. Dally, Reverend Joseph W. *Woodbridge and Vicinity: The Story of a New Jersey Township*. p. 6.
2. Ludewig, Dorothy F.D. *Timely Told Tales of Woodbridge Township, Tercentenary Edition—1669–1969*. p. 11.
3. Hester, Tom. "A Tragic Chapter." The *Star-Ledger*. 15 February 2001.
4. Clayton, W. Woodford. *History of Union and Middlesex Counties*. p. 555.
5. McCormick, Richard P. *New Jersey from Colony to State–1609-1789*. Vol. 1. pp. 23–24.

CHAPTER THREE

1. Dally, Reverend Joseph W. *Woodbridge and Vicinity: The Story of a New Jersey Township*. p. 79.
2. Jamison, Wallace N. *Religion in New Jersey: A Brief History*. Vol. 13. p. 34.
3. Dally, Reverend Joseph W. *Woodbridge and Vicinity: The Story of a New Jersey Township*. p. 41.
4. Ibid., p. 17.
5. Gilman, C. Malcolm B. *Blazing Star: A New Jersey Privateer in the American Revolution*. p. 4.

CHAPTER FOUR

1. Dally, Reverend Joseph W. *Woodbridge and Vicinity: The Story of a New Jersey Township*. p. 240.
2. Ibid., p. 206.
3. Cunningham, John T. *New Jersey: America's Main Road*. p. 67
4. Fisher, Edgar Jacob. *New Jersey as a Royal Province, 1738–1776*. Vol. XLI. pp. 412–413.
5. Ibid., p. 423.

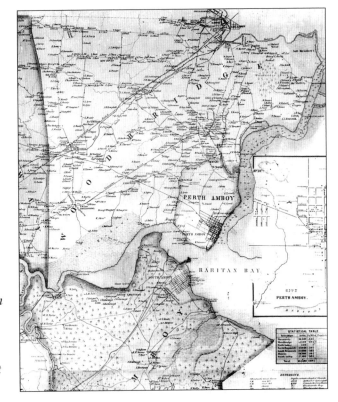

EARLY WOODBRIDGE. As shown on this map, which was probably drawn about 1850, the township was considerably larger when it was originally settled, with Lower Rahway, Metuchen, Carteret, and parts of Edison Township within its boundaries. Although adjacent to the township, Perth Amboy was never part of Woodbridge.

WOODBRIDGE, ENGLAND. This contemporary watercolor depicts the waterfront of the Suffolk County town where many of the early township settlers originally lived.

CHAPTER FIVE

1. Hester, Tom. "Center of the Storm, New Jersey and the American Revolution." p. 3.
2. Dally, Reverend Joseph W. *Woodbridge and Vicinity: The Story of a New Jersey Township*. p. 242.
3. Hester, Tom. "Center of the Storm, New Jersey and the American Revolution." p. 11.
4. Stillman, G.W. *Battle of Short Hills in the Revolutionary War*. Notes from a lecture given to the Historical Association of Woodbridge Township, May 2002.
5. Dally, Reverend Joseph W. *Woodbridge and Vicinity: The Story of a New Jersey Township*. p. 228.
6. Dally, Reverend Joseph W. *Woodbridge and Vicinity: The Story of a New Jersey Township*. p. 253.
7. Ibid., p. 254.
8. Ibid., p. 285.

CHAPTER SIX

1. Kreger, John M. "Woodbridge and Its Clays." The *Independent-Leader*. 11 June 1964.

2. Ibid.

3. Reif, Rita. "Art Section." The *New York Times*. 27 January 2002. p. 39.

4. Clayton, W. Woodford. *History of Union and Middlesex Counties*. p. 583.

5. Kreger, John M. "Woodbridge and Its Clays." The *Independent-Leader*. 11 June 1964.

6. Wolk, Ruth. *The History of Woodbridge, New Jersey*. pp. 48–49.

7. Kreger, John M. "Woodbridge and Its Clays." The *Independent-Leader*. 11 June 1964.

8. Holtzman, Elias. "Bombs Proliferate Area's Terra Cotta Collection." *Home News Tribune*. 17 January 2002. p. D3.

CHAPTER SEVEN

1. Clayton, W. Woodford. *History of Union and Middlesex Counties*. p. 584.

2. Schopp, Paul W. Electronic communication to the New Jersey History Listserv, 7 February 2002.

3. Lender, Mark Edward. *Middlesex Water Company: A Business History*. p. 201.

CHAPTER EIGHT

1. Wolk, Ruth. "History of the Township School System." The *Independent Leader*. *c*. 1940.

2. Ibid.

3. Perry, Tex, and David T. Miller Sr. *A History of Iselin, New Jersey*. p. 17.

CHAPTER TEN

1. Pattison, Mary. *Colonia Yesterday: A Biographical History of a Small Community*. p. 15.

2. The Women's Project of New Jersey. *Past and Promise, Lives of New Jersey Women*. p. 176. (Information on Mary Pattison written by Harriet Hyman Alonso and Janet Crawford.)

3. Ibid, p. 176–177.

4. Lawlor, Julia. "Curry and Saris Spice a Typical Suburb." The *New York Times*. 21 April 2002. Real Estate Section. p. 5.

5. Wolk, Ruth. *The History of Woodbridge, New Jersey*. p. 168.

CHAPTER TWELVE

1. Miller, David T., Sr. *Colonia: a Tercentenary Community*. p. 110.

2. Ludewig, Dorothy F.D. *Timely Told Tales of Woodbridge Township, Tercentenary Edition—1669–1969*. Foreword by Martha J. Morrow, p. IV.

3. Dally, Reverend Joseph W. *Woodbridge and Vicinity: The Story of a New Jersey Township*. pp. 294-295.

4. Woodbridge High School. *History of Woodbridge Township* (adapted from Leon McElroy's materials). p. 4.

5. Breckenridge, Amy E. *Disappearing Landmarks of Woodbridge*. p. 17.

6. Ludewig, Dorothy F.D. *Timely Told Tales of Woodbridge Township, Tercentenary Edition—1669–1969*. p. 138.

7. Wolk, Ruth. *The History of Woodbridge, New Jersey*. p. 181.

"Big Paddy" c. 1910. Patrick Cullinane, seated here in a presumably borrowed car, holds the honor of being the town's first policeman.

BIBLIOGRAPHY

Baird, Donald. "Medial Cretaceous Carnivorous Dinosaur and Footprints from New Jersey." *The Mosasaur: The Journal of the Delaware Valley Paleontological Society.* October 1989.

Branin, M. Lelyn. *The Early Makers of Handcrafted Earthenware and Stoneware in Central and Southern New Jersey.* Cranbury, NJ: Associated University Presses (Fairleigh Dickinson University), 1988.

Breckenridge, Amy E. *Disappearing Landmarks of Woodbridge.* Woodbridge: Privately published, 1946.

Clayton, W. Woodford, ed. *History of Union and Middlesex Counties, New Jersey.* Philadelphia: Everts and Peck, 1882.

Cunningham, John T. *New Jersey: America's Main Road.* Revised edition. Garden City, NY: Doubleday and Company, Inc., 1976.

Dally, Reverend Joseph W. *Woodbridge and Vicinity: The Story of a New Jersey Township.* Lambertville, NJ: Hunterdon House, 1989. (Originally published 1873.)

Detweiler, Frederic C. *War in the Countryside: The Battle and Plunder of the Short Hills, New Jersey, June, 1777.* Plainfield, NJ: Interstate Printing Corporation, 1977.

Fisher, Edgar Jacob. *New Jersey as a Royal Province, 1738–1776, Vol. XLI of Studies in History, Economics and Public Law.* New York: Columbia University, 1911. (Reprinted in 1967 by AMS Press, Inc., New York.)

Gallagher, William B. *When Dinosaurs Roamed New Jersey.* New Brunswick, NJ: Rutgers University Press, 1977.

Gilman, C. Malcolm B. *Blazing Star: A New Jersey Privateer in the American Revolution.* South Brunswick, NJ and New York: A.S. Barnes and Company, 1974.

———. *The Story of the Jersey Blues.* Red Bank, NJ: Arlington Laboratory for Clinical and Historical Research, 1962.

Hester, Tom. "Center of the Storm: New Jersey and the American Revolution." Newark, NJ: The *Star-Ledger*, 2001.

Hester, Tom. "A Tragic Chapter." The *Star-Ledger*. 15 February 2001.

History of Methodism. (Manual and Directory of the Church). Woodbridge, NJ: 1902.

Jamison, Wallace N. *Religion in New Jersey: A Brief History*. Vol. 13. (The New Jersey Historical Series.) Princeton, NJ: D.Van Nostrand Company, Inc., 1964.

Jost, Edna Oberlies, and Margaret Krewinkel Jost. *What's Cooking in Woodbridge, New Jersey: An Historical Sampler 1664–1964*. Woodbridge: Woodbridge Publishing Company, 1964.

Karasik, Gary, and Anna M. Aschkenes. *Middlesex County: Crossroads of History*. Sun Valley, CA: American History Press, 1999.

Kraft, Herbert C. *The Lenape—Archaeology, History and Ethnography*. Newark, NJ: New Jersey Historical Society, 1986.

Kreger, John M. *Township of Woodbridge, New Jersey, 1669–1781*. Colonia, NJ: St. George Press, Inc., 1976.

Kreger, John M. "Woodbridge and Its Clays." The *Independent-Leader*. 11 June 1964.

Krull, Reverend Michael G. *A History of the Parish of Our Lady of Peace*. Fords, NJ: 1994.

Lawlor, Julia. "Curry and Saris Spice a Typical Suburb." The *New York Times*. 21 April 2002.

Lender, Mark Edward. *Middlesex Water Company: A Business History*. Metuchen, NJ: The Upland Press, 1994.

Ludewig, Dorothy F.D. "Fords Yesterday and Today." Woodbridge, NJ: *Independent-Leader* Publishing Company, 1964.

Ludewig, Dorothy F.D. *Timely Told Tales of Woodbridge Township, Tercentenary Edition—1669–1969*. Woodbridge: Woodbridge Township Board of Education, 1970.

Miers, Earl Schenck. *Where the Raritan Flows*. New Brunswick, NJ: Rutgers University Press, 1964.

Miller, David T. Sr. *Colonia: A Tercentenary Community*. Colonia, NJ: St. George Press, 1971.

Morrow, Martha J., and Edward E. Baker, eds. *History, First Presbyterian Church, Woodbridge, New Jersey, 300th Anniversary*, 1675–1975. Woodbridge: First Presbyterian Church, 1975.

Myers, Patty Barthell. *Ancestors and Descendants of Lewis Ross Freeman with Related Families*. Based partially on the work of Freeman Worth Gardner and Willis Freeman. San Antonio, TX: Penobscot Press, 1995.

Nelson, Philip Noe. Unpublished family history.

Newman, Simon P. *Parades and the Politics of the Street, Festive Culture in the Early American Republic*. Philadelphia: University of Pennsylvania Press, 1997.

Pattison, Mary. *Colonia Yesterday: A Biographical History of a Small Community*. Colonia, NJ: The Junto, 1949.

Perry, Tex, and David T. Miller Sr. *A History of Iselin, New Jersey*. Colonia, NJ: St. George Press, 1975.

Reif, Rita. Art Section. The *New York Times*. 27 January 2002.

Schopp, Paul W. Electronic Communication to the New Jersey History Listserv. 7 February 2002.

Stillman, G.W. "Battle of Short Hills in the Revolutionary War." Lecture. May 2002.

Troeger, Virginia Bergen, and Robert J. McEwen. *Images of America: Woodbridge.* Vols. I and II. Dover, NH: Arcadia Publishing, 1997 and 1999.

Widmer, Kemble. *The Geology and Geography of New Jersey.* Vol. 19. (The New Jersey Historical Series). Princeton: D. Van Nostrand Company, Inc., 1964.

Wolk, Ruth. *The History of Woodbridge, New Jersey.* Woodbridge: 1970.

———. "History of the Township School System (a series)." The *Independent Leader.* 1940.

The Women's Project of New Jersey. *Past and Promise, Lives of New Jersey Women.* Metuchen, NJ, and London: The Scarecrow Press, 1990. (Information on Mary Pattison written by Harriet Hyman Alonso and Janet Crawford.)

Woodbridge High School. *History of Woodbridge Township* (adapted from Leon McElroy's materials). Woodbridge, NJ: Woodbridge High School, 1955.

Woodbridge High School. *History of Education, Woodbridge Township, 1664–1964.* Woodbridge: Woodbridge High School, 1964.

WELL-KNOWN COUPLE C. 1976. John and Evelyn Kreger were active for many years in township organizations and at the First Presbyterian Church. Mrs. Kreger died in the 1990s at the age of 100. (Jean Kreger Jost)

INDEX

RIVERWATCH, C. 1995. Volunteers gather debris along one of Woodbridge's waterways. (Ernie Oros)